MOTION SICKNESS

A MEMOIR

DAVID LAYTON

Macfarlane Walter & Ross

Toronto

Macfarlane Walter & Ross
37A Hazelton Avenue
Toronto, Canada M5R 2E3

Distributed in Canada by:
General Distribution Services Ltd.

Distributed in the United States by:
General Distribution Services Inc.
85 River Rock Drive, Suite 202
Buffalo, New York 14207
Toll-free Tel. 1-800-805-1083
Toll-free Fax 1-800-481-6207
Email gdsinc@genpub.com

Canadian Cataloguing in Publication Data

Layton, David, 1964–
Motion sickness: a memoir

ISBN 1-55199-039-3

1. Layton, Irving 1912- – Family.   2. Layton, David, 1964-   – Childhood
and youth.   3. Poets, Canadian (English) – 20th century – Biography.*
I. Title

PS8523.A95Z75 1999   C811'.54   C99-932002-5
PR9199.3.L35Z75 1999

Macfarlane Walter & Ross gratefully acknowledges financial support
for its publishing program from the Canada Council for the Arts,
the Ontario Arts Council, and the Government of Canada through the Book
Publishing Industry Development Program.

Printed and bound in Canada

TO MY WIFE, ANN

A child hopes for parents who will be inconspicuous.
AUBERON WAUGH

CONTENTS

Acknowledgments

A C K N O W L E D G M E N T S

Thanks to Gary Ross, Jon Ennis, and Frances Checkley

for their help and support, and to Ian Robinson, Neil Sabin,

and Claudia Cano de Jaime at the Acapulco Princess Hotel

for giving me the opportunity to finish this book.

And special thanks to my mother, with love.

THE PRINCE OF MOROCCO

Towards the end of spring my mother began to cry. Her tears came with the season. They started as a few sobs. Then, as the flowers bloomed, and the trees swelled in size, her tears burst their banks. My father fled to the high-water mark of his attic and I to the underwater estuary of the basement. I drowned, my father floated. Such was the arrangement.

My father had the ability to manufacture his own optimism. When things were going particularly badly, as they were now, he'd bellow into the phone and proclaim to anyone who would listen that things "couldn't be better." He simply marched to his own drummer and with time, one couldn't help but join his parade. His insistence upon normalcy was a grand feat, worthy of admiration. The reason he was going to Rome alone, he said, was that it was necessary to stir the creative juices.

"Mix the juices, is more like it," my mother countered.

In response, my father asked what was for dinner. If the issue wasn't properly spelled out, why not claim illiteracy?

"You're not going alone," my mother screamed, "you're going with that fat sycophant of yours. She gets your private parts and I'm left laundering the underwear!"

This kind of talk disturbed my father. He was not fond of prurient language invading his domestic setting. There were, after all, standards of behaviour to be upheld.

"Listen, Aviva, I can't have this ridiculous conversation with you." When he began to walk away he added, just for good measure, "You're insane."

Being ten years old, I didn't really know what creative juices were, but I did know that there were two tickets booked, and that one of them was for a mysterious woman. I'd become accustomed to my father's denials. When he'd fart in the car and my mother and I were forced to paddle in fresh air with our hands, he was insistent that no smell could be detected. The laughter his denials once brought forth had, over the years, been transformed into outright hostility.

"But Irving, you did fart."

My father never offered a denial that was strong enough to be construed as defensive. His face never reddened in embarrassment. He simply had not farted and any continuation of the discussion was irrelevant.

One day my father disappeared from the house. His ascent to the attic was unstoppable; he'd gone up and out. I never saw the suitcases being packed for Rome or heard the cab come to take him away. There weren't any farewells, just an absence to let me know that my father had flown the coop. Admittedly, my mother's mood improved. She still let out a yelp every now and then, but the waters had receded and I could surface from my basement underworld.

Like my father, my mother spent a great deal of time on the phone making proclamations. But unlike my father's, hers were apocalyptic. "He's impossible. I've decided to leave him," she'd sob. It was too late, I thought. He'd already left her.

That summer we made our way from Toronto to London and I entered another basement. It belonged to Nada, an ex-Montrealer who'd moved to London years earlier and created a kind of salon in her apartment. This being England, the salon was in a basement flat that smelled of mould and gas leaks. During our stay, an assortment of odd-looking creatures made their way into and out of her apartment. Bookish Swedes, American actors, British hippies, dreadlocked Jamaicans — the list was endless. Her apartment was also known as the Canadian Embassy. Every summer, Canadians flocked to her place, with the lingering horror of winter and cultural starvation on their faces. They were often the most excited and excitable of the bunch.

As a collector of people, Nada rightly stayed away from debasing her collection. She had a deep admiration for my father and understood that great men, like priceless objects, have flaws which only heighten their worth. This allowed her to be sympathetic to my mother's pain without being disloyal to my father, and I suspected that this was the only form of compassion my mother would have accepted, even when she was filled with bitterness.

I slept in Nada's bedroom, on a couch stacked with

pillows and brightly coloured blankets. I lay there like a Persian prince, secure and warm with my two mothers, and listened to their conversation drifting in from the kitchen.

"It's all over," my mother said. Her tone had changed. Up till now such proclamations were filled with either hysteria or deep resignation, but now I detected a weary humour. I heard laughter.

"Come to Morocco with Diana and me," said Nada, but my mother continued as if she hadn't heard.

"No really, the man's impossible. He's like a child. No, he *is* a child."

A screech from the kettle stopped the conversation and I heard its sigh as it was lifted from the flame.

"I worry about David," said Nada. Hearing my name, I opened my eyes.

"In the fight for attention they're like two children, and poor David always loses. Irving's roar is louder."

So my father was my brother. How could that be? I remembered how I'd once caught my father pissing in the sink. This was strange since the toilet was no more than two feet away. But there he was, balanced on his toes, peeing into the enamel washbowl.

Seeing me standing there at the door, he'd let out a fitful "Hello, son!" and quickly pushed his pecker back into his underwear and turned on the faucet. He'd looked rather shocked as he tried to drain the urine from the basin. I would have thought more about his odd behaviour if I hadn't been so fascinated by his penis. It looked like an ancient animal.

"Daddy pissed in the sink," I said to my mother the next day. She was furious.

"I can't pull that boy away from your tit!" was my father's response. I tried to believe that his concern was for my welfare, but I felt it had more to do with his own.

"Don't blame your son," said my mother.

"I'm not. I'm blaming you."

"At least *he* uses the toilet."

No, this man was no brother of mine, I thought. But if he wasn't my brother, he wasn't exactly my father either. We were rivals for my mother's affection. Except that I peed in the toilet — just as my mother had told me to do.

"How would you like to go to Morocco?" my mother asked me the next morning. Her pretense of democratic principles was annoying if only because I repeatedly fell for it. *How would I like to go to Morocco?* I didn't know where it was. I didn't even know *what* it was.

"I don't want to go."

This did not produce the desired effect. My mother went on about what a great trip we'd have with "Auntie" Nada and her friend Diana.

"And Jasmine will be coming," she added.

Jasmine was Nada's daughter. I was supposed to be elated by the notion that she would be accompanying us. Nada and my mother liked to foster the idea that we were brother and sister, an idea which would only be abolished on the day of our marriage to each other. And that day, they liked to say, was not far off. This troubled me. We'd once played doctor together, but my authority to examine her seemed to be undermined by her greater size and age. I may have done the examination, but she was the one to tell me where to poke around.

"I don't want to go."

"Well," my mother answered, "first we'll go to

Spain — then we'll go to Morocco. Why don't we try it for a bit and see if we like it."

This trip to Morocco represented a very disturbing trend. We'd been arriving at Nada's London flat for as long as I could remember. It was always the same. My mother's tearful calls from Toronto, her night-long discussions over Nada's kitchen table, the shoddy declarations of freedom. Such was the case every year. But Morocco? Normally after a few days in London we'd be off, eventually ending up in Molyvos, a small village on the Greek island of Lesbos. There my mother would search for a house and fix it up. Then, when everything was in order, my father would arrive, bags in hand, and we'd all settle in for a long, warm summer.

"But what about Greece?" I asked.

She hesitated before answering. I could see the pain and knew it was something I could work on.

"Not this year."

"Why not?" I asked. It was a genuine question. After all, my father's absence had never been a barrier before.

"Because this year we're going to Morocco," she answered. And then she walked away as if to declare that her own absence was equal to that of my father's.

"I've made a mistake."

Once again my mother was crying. Two days of walking around Madrid, and we'd sunk into a miserable depression. Her tears were infectious and soon I was at it myself. We had concluded that the Spaniards were not as friendly, the smell not as intoxicating, the light not as idyllic as in "our" Greece.

Our tears dropped on the carpeted floor of our

hotel room. It was a magnificent room, all carved stone and gilded plaster, superior in every way to the crumbling concrete pensions we'd inhabited in Athens. But Greece, we had convinced ourselves, was home.

I was far too young for such nostalgia, but there I was waxing eloquent about the marvels and pleasures of Greece. My mother's weakness had given me an opening, a last shot at getting our asses out of this place and away from an unsure future. Without Nada by her side, my mother was weakening.

"Let's go to Greece," I said. "We can do it."

"Would you like to go?" she asked. The answer to this question was so self-evident it could only mean she needed a hook to hang her decision on.

"It's where we belong," I said mournfully. Below the hotel window spread a long boulevard where old men were selling bright balloons. "We should leave right now."

My mother's ability to envelop me in her own confusion saved her from the worst ravages of self-absorption. I was always included. Even better, I was consulted.

"I think we should wait until we meet Nada, and then we'll see."

There was nothing more to be said, although we kept on talking about how miserable we were. This was our bond. Such topics, I knew, were alien to my father. He was never miserable. At least that's what he said and I couldn't help but believe him. He certainly would not be sobbing in any hotel room. My mother and I, on the other hand, were always left in his wake and our decisions were reactive to his own — either we followed directly behind him or we cut away and made for choppy seas. But always we were pulled. My mother just couldn't let go of the rope.

We met Nada in Pamplona. According to my mother, it was the "running of the bulls" that attracted all these people. This was what I knew of the festival: there were bulls out there, they ran through the streets, and you had to avoid them at all costs. Not quite comprehending the notion of containment, I could never be sure that a herd of bulls was not about to rush round the corner. It would certainly explain all those drunken men in the streets — the end was near and it could come at any moment.

Sangria, a wine stew made with chunks of fruit for flavour and nourishment, was, I learned, the main culprit. My mother and Nada never seemed to be far from a wine bowl themselves. They were always in the main square, holding court in the bright sunshine, their chairs tucked under the shade of an umbrella. For the most part I left them alone or they left me alone — I was never sure which — and I ended up meandering through the streets, where I'd keep an eye out for angry bulls.

Anyone could run with the bulls in Pamplona, even the drunks who staggered about. Police were posted at every gate to dissuade men from running. But they also had another assignment — to prevent those who had failed to listen to their wise counsel from exiting. I was forever wondering if I had passed through the gate by accident.

Leaving Pamplona with Nada and Jasmine in tow, we headed to Ibiza to pick up Diana. Diana was an actress given to dramatic displays, who turned even the most banal remarks into exclamations. We all stayed in a house owned by a man with dank hair and rotten teeth. Each night Diana would belt out a series of screams from inside his bedroom. In the morning, fascinated, I'd wait for her to emerge from the room, her hair like a wild thyme bush. Much to the consternation of everyone else, she never appeared the least bit embarrassed. Nada told me that because she was an actress it was in her blood to perform.

The man with bad teeth also made unpleasant noises, but these came outside the bedroom. He'd moan every time a tooth fired up. I'd watch him reach for his tooth drops, a noxious red liquid that he kept on a mantelpiece not more than three feet from where I slept. I couldn't help feeling that his pain was more genuine than her pleasure.

Our passage from Spain to Morocco was conducted at night. An entire civilization was being transported over water. The deck was full of men, rope, wood, and steel. Our car was somewhere down in the bowels of the boat and we were up on the deck, in the wind and smoke of a foreign country. We were outnumbered, overwhelmed. It seemed to me that we'd entered a world full of men and danger. The music sounded dangerous. The sea looked dangerous. The food smelled dangerous. I needed to get back into the car.

Unfortunately my mother didn't seem worried, just excited. My trust in her had been rapidly diminishing these last few weeks. The men on the boat didn't look at her, or me, or Nada; they were too involved in playing cards, in watching their possessions, in talking. But I was convinced they were thinking of us, and that their thoughts weren't pleasant.

Nada's outfit, all purple and flowing, was beginning to make sense to me. On her visits to Canada, she looked like some over-exotic flower. But now, under the naked light bulbs strung across the boat, she was clearly a part of whatever it was we were moving towards. The Moroccans looked thin and dirty compared with Nada, but I got the feeling that this did not remove her from them. She was their queen. My instinct was to stick close to her.

"It's so *hot!*"

A typically emphatic statement of the obvious from Diana. We were crammed into an old VW Beetle, driving through the desert. The sweltering air had chapped our lips and dried out our nostrils. My mother's leg felt like a heater — I pushed it away. Jasmine was passed out with her mouth open while Nada, who was sitting in the front seat, kept turning her head to assure us that we'd be in the mountains soon. I already knew what they were called. The Atlas Mountains. I'd once seen a picture of a man called Atlas, wrapped in a lion's skin, holding the entire world on his shoulders. Even with his strength, it seemed a burden.

The mountains soon lifted us above the heat and along with rivers and trees came men standing on the road yelling at our car.

"Hashish! Hashish!"

The farther we went, the larger the bags they held in their hands.

"It must be dried camel shit," Jasmine said. She had fully recovered from her previous torpor and was now staring wide-eyed at the men who shouted at us. Her comments sparked a debate which made me feel that Jasmine, at sixteen, was an equal of the other women in the car. While everyone seemed concerned about the substance that was being offered, I was far more concerned with those doing the offering. A few were no older than I was, and all of them looked desperate.

Cars began to appear on the previously empty road. They'd flash their headlights as they sped past and then disappear around the next bend. Soon there were groups of men on the road, some holding up the brown bags, others stepping out onto the road and making a circle with their thumb and index finger.

"Zero! Zero!"

A car pulled up alongside us. The tinted window in the front seat slid down and a man began to yell.

"Zero! Zero!" he shouted. He made the same sign as the others and placed his hands over his eyes as if he were peering through glasses. He looked mad.

"What does he want?" Diana asked. Nobody knew, so my mother and Nada told her to keep driving.

"We should stop."

"Don't stop," Jasmine pleaded.

"I can't keep driving. I *can't!*" And then, before anyone could say another word, Diana put her foot on the brake. The other car pulled up in front of us. Diana left the engine on, but even so it seemed very quiet while we waited for the man to make his way over.

"What do you want?" Diana snapped. This, I knew, was the kind of approach Nada disapproved of. In Morocco, she said, one had to be graceful and considerate. At all times. She had, in a very delicate way, pressed this point upon Diana, whose black mood seemed to deepen the farther we went into Morocco. There was, in Nada's advice, a sense that if you weren't polite, there could be ... repercussions.

"Why didn't you stop?" the man asked.

"You speak very good English," said Nada.

"I spent some time in England," the man answered. "Would you like to visit my farm?"

The question was so unexpected that the women laughed, but just as he had neglected to consider Diana's hostile question so he also failed to notice their laughter. "I think you will enjoy it. It is not too far from here." The man addressed himself primarily to Nada but he did not fail to look each of us in the eye. It was oddly comforting.

Nada thanked him profusely but said that we had other arrangements.

"You will not find anything better," he answered matter-of-factly. "You can stay for a day or a week. For however long you feel."

"Why is everybody shouting 'Zero, zero'?" Diana demanded to know.

"'Zero zero' is for the best hashish." The man made two circles with his hands and smiled beatifically. "You won't find it here. My name is Mohammed. Come, follow me."

As the man walked back to his car, Jasmine noticed that it was a Mercedes-Benz. Incredibly, this fact appeared to pacify any doubts either Diana or Nada entertained. My mother, who had long ago learned to sense my fears, made it known that she was rather worried. But her protest was, in my opinion, weak.

Diana diligently followed the black car as it sped down the winding mountain roads. We slowed for a wedding procession making its way through a village and spotted the bride and groom. The man in the Mercedes leaned his head out the window. "Berbers!" he shouted. This excited everyone in the car. My mother waved at the crowd.

An hour later we were halted by several men in army uniform. The man in the black car called it a "checkpoint" but it looked to me more like a border crossing; a long metal arm stretched out over the road, separating one side from the other. It was my hope that the guards would haul off everyone but my mother and me, but after inspecting our passports they opened the gate and let us through. Strangely, a gigantic hotel, pink and tall, stood just to the other side of the roadblock. Expensive-looking cars littered the landscaped driveway. Between the space made by the hotel and a manicured hedgerow, I could make out a swimming pool. Just as I closed my eyes and imagined myself behind the hotel's comforting walls, we turned off the road.

"Where the hell is he going?" Diana shouted.

"Can't we go to the hotel?" I pleaded.

My mother began to feel that this was a good idea and, after half an hour of bumping along the rocky ground, so did Nada. The car we had followed was now a long way off, so far off that all we were following was the dust kicked up by its tires.

"If anybody would care to tell me how to find the road again, I'll turn," pronounced Diana.

There were two large hills ahead of us, their contours already blurred by the dim evening light. Behind us was the wide sweep of flat land that we had been travelling on, somewhere further back was the road, and further back still, the hotel. Diana turned on the headlights. To our surprise, a village appeared in front of us.

"You will find our home comfortable."

This village was more than comfortable, I thought. There were chickens and women, two emblems of domesticity, so it must be safe. A large tray of couscous was brought to us minutes after we entered the room. We sat cross-legged around a wooden table and plunged our hands into the steaming grain. Nada informed Mohammed that it was the best couscous she'd ever eaten.

"It's made with butter. And 'zero zero.'"

"Zero couscous," Nada repeated. She started laughing.

"Zero couscous," he answered.

Everyone, including myself, mouthed the magic words. Jasmine stood up and started dancing. "Zero couscous, zero couscous," she sang.

I laughed so hard my mother put me to bed. We were all in one long room, with piles of carpets and pillows to lie on. Soon everyone was reclining in the soft darkness of lighted candles. I could feel the earth spin from top to bottom. No point trying to hold it steady like the giant with the world on his shoulders, so I let it spin me around. All the way around. Sometimes the revolutions slowed down and stopped altogether.

Now I was upside down.

Now I was asleep.

The village we had arrived at so late at night was in the Katama Valley, where, as Mohammed told us, even the flies were stoned. In the daylight, the hills and valleys were green with marijuana plants. We were on a farm where the main nourishment came from a noxious smoke that everyone sucked into their bodies. I spent my days walking through the fields with my new village friend, a boy who breathed heavily and had sweaty palms. Like the rest of the villagers, he was both muscular and malnourished. We threw stones across dry riverbeds and periodically popped little hashish pellets into our mouths.

Sometimes I followed him to the village school where a collection of ragged children of every size and age stared glassy-eyed at the teacher. The animals I'd seen were in no better shape.

Jasmine explained it all to me one day.

"They need people to come and take the hashish away from here."

"Is that what we're going to do?" I asked.

"No, we don't have any money. But they hope that

when we return we'll talk to people who do."

I was relieved to hear this. There were three Italians in the next room who spent their days nervously watching villagers place slabs of compressed hashish into the lining of their suitcases. It was a delicate job, and when the men had finished they ran their fingernails over the seamless stitches and smiled. The next day the suitcases were gone and so were the Italians.

On my suggestion, my mother and I took a walk through the village. I wanted to confess my fears. I told her that I wanted to stop feeling so strange, that I feared I was becoming "addicted." I thought this was a mature thing to say. My mother laughed at my words but her pitch was too high. I knew then that my attempt at being an adult had failed.

Nevertheless, we left the next day, headed for Casablanca. The countryside we travelled through was softer than before, flooded with yellow light and mountain lakes. After a day of driving, we stopped at another small village to visit some friends of Nada's. A servant greeted us at the door and led us to the living room where a father and his son were sitting on a threadbare carpet, barefoot and cross-legged. They were American.

"Look," Nada said, "a friend for David." I felt there was something mean about her remark. She was pointing out my needs to strangers.

"Someone your own age to play with," my mother said with forced delight.

But the boy I was to play with had not lifted his head, or even noticed our arrival. His only movement came from his nimble fingers, which were spinning a joint. The noise of our arrival was quickly replaced by silent obedience as we took our places on the rug to watch as he lit a match. He waited patiently for the flare to turn into fire and then, with a delicacy I'd never before seen in someone my own age, set his creation alight and inhaled deeply. I turned to face my mother, but her eyes were fixed on his. From the look on her face I could tell that her horror was compromised by fascination.

My encounter with Casablanca started with my nostrils. A relentless smell of damp stone, petrol fumes, and charred meat entered the car through the rolled-down windows. I could hear the ocean, then see flecks of water spray the night air as the dark liquid crashed down on boulders and the seawall. We turned off a wide boulevard, passed a restaurant where men stared at us, and finally moved through a series of narrow streets. The car pushed up a small incline in the road, turned into a driveway, and came to a stop. In front of us was a "proper" house, on a quiet street. Unlike the places where we had been staying, there was an immediate sense of order.

After greeting Nada's friend Jos, who lived here, my mother put me quickly to bed, tucked me in, and kissed my sweaty brow.

"Night, night, sleep tight, and don't let the bedbugs bite," she whispered. It was her way of sending me back home, back to my bedroom where everything had a place, and where I knew all the places. She turned off the light and left me. In the darkness everything could be arranged according to my needs. It was not hard to banish the foreign smells and think: "I'm home, in my own bed. The wall of cork where I pin my drawings is just behind me, my basket of toys is in the corner, there are two windows over-looking my street, and just at the foot of the bed is the door where a hallway leads past my parents' bedroom." If

I tried hard I could even hear the hum of our refrigerator.

It took several days for my fever to break. When I awoke there was light pouring into my room. I lay in bed, comfortable and exhausted. It was the first real bedroom I'd been in since Madrid. My bed was high off the ground and there was a small table against the opposite wall with several framed photographs pointed in my direction. Everything was calm and quiet.

"David?"

The wall beside me was slatted like a wooden shutter.

"Jasmine?"

"Are you feeling better?" she asked.

"Yes," I answered and propped my head against some pillows and asked her what she was doing.

"I've been sick too," she said.

"Where is everybody?"

"They've gone out for the afternoon, but they'll be back soon."

I realized that Jasmine was lying on a bed just like mine. We shared this wall and much more. Her illness had made her a child again. We spent the day talking and sleeping and sometimes, when I knew she was awake, I would stick a finger through the wooden slats to feel the comforting strokes of her hand.

I could tell the minute my mother entered the room that something was up. Her excitement over my recovery was far too pronounced to be healthy. It had to have come from other sources. In the living room, I heard Nada and Jos talking about a prince.

"What prince?" I asked.

"Bashir, the Prince of Morocco," my mother

answered, placing a cup of tea at my side. "We're all going to have dinner with him tonight."

"Is Jasmine coming?" I asked.

In front of me was a dining room with real chairs and a candle which sat on the middle of the table. I didn't want to leave this house.

"Can't we stay?"

"We can't stay here tonight," my mother answered. "Even Jos is coming with us."

I looked at the woman whose house I was staying in. She was my mother's age. I liked her because I liked her house, but I also had a dreadful sense that she was somehow responsible for conjuring up this mysterious Prince of Morocco.

That night we returned to the seawall, with its crashing waves and strewn boulders. We went to a restaurant with elegantly set tables and flickering candles. A band of musicians was playing soft music, while men in white uniforms escorted people to their tables. The prince was waiting for us. He stood up when we arrived and waited for us all to be seated before resuming his position. I caught a glimpse of his knee-high boots, silver belt, and earring. On anyone else it would have looked like a Halloween costume. On Bashir, with his black hair and almond-coloured skin, it lent him a handsome authority. He was the kind of person who could seat himself at the head of the table, even if it was round. My mother sat down beside him and, to my surprise, conversation between them was immediate and familiar.

"Do you like to ride bikes?" the prince asked me somewhat later in the evening.

I told him that I had a bicycle.

"Then you must come to my palace in Rabat and ride with my son. He is your age."

My mother was enthralled by the idea.

"Oh!" she exclaimed. "That would be fun, wouldn't it, David?" She clapped her hands together.

I thought to myself: My mother is fucking delirious.

The night wore on. I cleared a small space for myself on the table and dropped my head onto the tablecloth. The musicians played a last song before tucking their instruments into metal cases. Without interrupting my mother's words, the prince lifted his arm and snapped his fingers. The musicians opened their cases and resumed playing.

In Rabat, my mother escorted me to the palace. And through it. Although several men were leading us past guarded gates and corridors, my mother seemed to have anticipated their sudden changes of direction. Each time we passed some precious object that sparkled she squeezed my arm.

I quickly concluded that the palace was not simply a very large house. It was a city hiding within another city. Rabat circled around the palace walls but never broke through. My mother had somehow found the magic potion that allowed us to walk through walls.

The prince was waiting for us, just as he had been in the restaurant, only now he was seated on a divan and the distractions which had partially diverted his attention from my mother the night before had been removed. He said a great many things in a very short time, but while his words scattered about the room his eyes were focused on my mother. And although his eyes sparkled just as brightly as the precious objects, my mother neglected to squeeze my arm.

I was led away from the two of them by a servant

who took me down a long corridor and out into an enclosed courtyard. A boy was there. He failed to notice my presence but his disdain was so all-pervasive that I didn't take it personally. Several more servants emerged from the shadows wheeling out two miniature motorcycles. The son of the prince was helped onto his bike, the motor was ignited, and then he sped away. I was spun round the perimeter of the courtyard by one of the servants.

After twenty or so laps the prince's son became bored and left his bike standing in the courtyard. Everyone else followed his lead and eventually I was led into a room where broad-shouldered men in suits and sunglasses sat watching a televised soccer match.

I was returned to my mother in the early evening. Nada was now a palace member. So were Diana and Jasmine. "Our" prince, I was informed, was the Prince of Rice. Apparently he received money for every grain of rice purchased in the Kingdom of Morocco. This information diminished him somewhat in my eyes but my mother assured me, a little too strenuously I thought, that he was very high on the food chain. Upon receiving this information I began to look at food differently. Who was the Prince of Olives? The Prince of Fish?

"Do you like Leonard Cohen?" the prince asked. "He is my favourite musician."

"Actually," my mother answered, with only a short pause for modesty, "I know Leonard Cohen."

"You know Leonard Cohen!" This excited the prince, who leaped up from his cushion and promptly left the room.

"Maybe he's getting an album," Nada said.

Everyone broke into hysterics over the idea that the Prince of Morocco would be searching through a pile of records for a Leonard Cohen album but the laughter quickly dissolved when the lights went out. Our attention turned to an embroidered curtain in front of us. It was pulled back and there he was — the Prince of Morocco, sitting on a stool, cradling a guitar. A fully equipped band stood attentively behind him. The odd thing was that he looked like Leonard. But that was where all similarities ended. As the prince began to sing he adopted a mournful, Leonard-like countenance, which compelled my mother to place a hand firmly over her mouth to stop her giggles. Everyone in the room was trying desperately to prevent a mass outbreak of laughter. I felt like laughing too. In this room of divans and florid carpets Bashir, now warbling on about Suzanne, banished for one small moment the exuberant furniture and returned me to my home with its unadorned walls and square, clear windows.

It was at home that I'd heard Leonard sing; his voice had often woken me at night and I'd walk down the stairs and into my mother's lap, where it would lull me back to sleep. His songs had a narcotic effect on my parents; they sat and listened, a look of serenity on their faces, which stayed there even after Leonard had stopped singing. My father would shake his head — "Ah, Leonard, my boy . . ." — while my mother gently rocked me.

My mother wasn't rocking me now. Bashir failed to have that effect. And of course my father was nowhere to be seen; the prince didn't have the power to conjure him up.

Diana listened with growing irritation, squirming in her pillows, and when the prince finished his rendition of Leonard Cohen and took his applause from the audience Diana leaned forward to Nada and my mother.

"Christ," she said, "even the Prince of Morocco wants to be an artist."

That was the last time I saw Bashir. It was also the last I was to see of my mother for a while. Without warning, she deposited me unceremoniously in the middle of the Moroccan desert and then disappeared.

At the age of ten I discovered that "nowhere" had a very precise location. It resided in southern Morocco, a few kilometres from the town of Essaouira, and its epicentre was a five-foot boulder that rested on the edge of a dry riverbed. I had the privilege of visiting this auspicious landmark every day before lunch. From its top I would watch the occasional camel make its way across the baked earth. Sometimes a few dusty goats, their owner nowhere in sight, would visit, but they obviously found it as unpromising a place as I did, and soon left.

My hosts, Scott and Aaron, were two strange men who played chess in the evening and read during the afternoon. I was fed three meals a day and that, it seemed, was the only nourishment I could expect from them. This was not due to any concerted malice on their part. I suspected that they'd spent far too much time inhaling Moroccan desert dust and it had weighed down their lungs, making conversation sparse and muting all sound to a whisper. In this oppressive somnolence I'd consume my meal and then excuse myself and sit in the cool darkness of my room for the duration of the afternoon.

What was this place? It bore a faint but nonetheless disturbing similarity to a roadside motel. Beside the main house there was a line of concrete cells, each containing a door and a back wall slit to let in a few strands of outside light. Lying down on the mattress, watching a heat-drugged fly piss away the afternoon by bouncing off the walls, I was certain that my mother had checked me into this place for good. It was the end of the line.

I felt that my mother's neglect, unlike that of my current caregivers, wasn't benign but malignant. I'd been carted from Toronto to London and then to Spain, squeezed into a Beetle with four women and hurled towards Africa. A procession of bulls, speed addicts, deserts, peasants, islands, urban sophisticates, Italian drug dealers, Berbers, mountains, and palaces had passed by me until finally I'd been deposited with Canada's most famous homosexual author. Then she'd left. And here I was.

Scott Symons smoked a pipe. I distrusted pipe smokers, especially bearded ones, for reasons I could not adequately explain. My father had a fine set of pipes in his attic office and I'd often take them out of their wooden cradles one by one, grasping their bulbous ends with appreciation. When I put my nose to the crater I could smell the deliciously sour odour of spent tobacco. Yet those engineered volcanoes of my father's were all but extinct. He rarely smoked pipes and when he did, it never seemed to be one from his attic. Those ones just sat on his bookcase like trophies, a reminder of some past pleasure.

But Scott always had a pipe clenched firmly between his teeth. He'd sit there on the patio and stare out over the rock-strewn desert in silent contemplation. Every so often he'd loosen his jaw and reposition the pipestem. I'd hear it rattle against his teeth and then his muscles would contract and he'd snap down on it; an animal paw caught in a steel trap. His peaceful countenance was an act of aggression. He smouldered in that silence, just like every other pipe smoker I'd ever encountered. In short, I didn't like him.

His lover Aaron, who was younger than Scott and clean-shaven, was also prone to pipe smoking. I couldn't help thinking that his apparent tranquility derived from a form of severe depression. I would have commiserated with him if I hadn't suspected that his circumstances were caused by a terrible lack of resolve.

I'd first overheard Aaron's story during whispered conversations in the car. He'd come to Morocco on his honeymoon, but a chance encounter with the famous Canadian writer had completely transformed his life. Scott had fallen in love with him and persuaded him that he was gay, so Aaron's newly minted wife packed her bags and returned to Canada, leaving the two men together.

Being ten, I could understand the circumstances if not all the details. Marriage, homosexuality, passion, deviance, stealth: these things were like the morning cup of coffee I'd seen adults drinking. I could identify the liquid through everything but taste.

Aaron had been subsumed by a higher purpose, a greater will. The will of a writer. This was acknowledged — and implicitly admired — by the four women of my apocalypse who never ceased to dwell on Scott's magnificent deviance. From what I could understand, Scott hadn't merely discovered Aaron's true sexual nature — he had created it. No mere archaeologist digging for what lay beneath the sands, Scott, like my father, was the architect of his surroundings. The world would conform to his notions, be built to his specifications. It just took time.

My mother's respect for good stories was surpassed only by her respect for those who created them. That was why we were here, in Morocco. I was trapped by my mother's fantasy of escape.

A limousine visited Scott's scruffy patch of desert late one afternoon. The driver walked round the front of the car and opened the back door. The air quivered from the escaping cool air of the interior and out of this mirage stepped my mother, cool and rested. She looked like an apparition.

"Mommy!" I shouted and ran towards the shimmering bubble. She came forward and wrapped me in her arms.

"I've missed you," she said. Her words flooded me with relief, while at the same time provoking intense resentment. After all, I wasn't the one doing the leaving.

Before I had a chance to say another word, my mother began walking in the direction of Scott and Aaron, who both stood at the edge of the patio, a kind of cement island in a sea of sand and stone.

"Aviva, you look wonderful," Scott said, smiling through his beard.

Everyone was duly impressed by the sight of an American limousine with a driver, who could be seen polishing the black hood with a rag as we sat around the patio table. Scott and Aaron served food and asked questions. The answers my mother offered were in the shape of stories, some of which I had not only heard before but witnessed. Other pieces of information, all of them disturbing, were passed about.

"The prince wants to open diplomatic relations with Israel," my mother proclaimed.

"And you are to be Morocco's Jewish ambassador?" queried Scott.

"He's in love with the Jews," my mother said.

"Or a Jew," Scott replied.

My mother's life had become wonderfully ridiculous as opposed to merely ridiculous and so she laughed. That she could help precipitate peace in the Middle East did not seem impossible in a land where carpets could fly, stones could turn into gold, and Arab princes fell in love with Jews.

Back home, my father had also talked about Jews, peace, and Israel. From what I could understand, there could be no peace in the Middle East without his say-so. The prince was, most obviously, an interloper.

It was apparent to me that my mother had thoughts to the contrary, but the uneasiness I felt was reserved for more practical and immediate matters. I noticed that the discarded plates, littered with olive pits and small bones, had already been pushed to the centre of the table. It was time to leave and I waited for my mother's instructions.

"I have to go," she said. I followed her movements as she left the table and headed towards the car. Even as we passed my room, I could not imagine that I would be left behind.

The chauffeur was waiting. He displayed a mannered deference to her which I'd seen no other man before him ever do. How had my mother been able to command this man's attention so thoroughly? She was possessed of a power which extended far beyond the one she held over me. I watched as the chauffeur opened up the back door of the limousine and let the shimmering bubble reclaim my mother. She managed to wave goodbye before being pulled back inside.

When I returned to my room the small rucksack, which I had quickly packed during lunch, was standing to one side of the mattress. Just a short time ago, the rucksack had been the focus of my frenzied attention. Now it stood there, a soft silent lump on the floor, looking lost and abandoned. I pulled it towards me and cradled it in my arms. Then I peered inside. A striped T-shirt, some shorts, a pair of running shoes sat in its hold. I pushed my nose into these familiar belongings and inhaled. Nothing but a foreign smell reached me. I pushed the sack away and curled up on my mattress.

Nada came to fetch me a few days later. She took me to Essaouira, and then quickly left. Although she didn't say so, I felt her disappearance to be the work of the prince. Diana was nowhere in sight either: after her energetic screams in Spain she had begun to fade until finally there was nothing left of her.

I was placed under Jasmine's care. Two abandoned children — it had come to that. We shared a hotel room on the top floor of an old, cavernous building built around an interior courtyard. The room was decorated with sky blue tiles and Air France posters. Our view was inward; I could see men from the opposite side of the building looking out over the empty space. Their gaze never seemed to reach my side of the building. One man, several floors down, was smoking a cigarette. Several other men were leaning over the balcony, staring vacantly. They looked like pieces of laundry hung out to dry.

Most of the men in the hotel were Moroccan. With evening came the sound of plastic sandals scraping across marble floors as they made their way to the bathroom. A few coughs. The coughs of men. The mournful sounds of flushing toilets.

One night, Jasmine took me to see *The Exorcist*. As I lay in bed later that night, I waited anxiously for the trembling signs of evil. I imagined that evil had been locked away beneath the desert floor, until men had arrived to dig up the totem which lay beneath the sands. I had no doubt that the now-empty hole lay on the outskirts of this town, in Scott and Aaron's compound.

Jasmine had slipped out when she thought I was sleeping, and I spent the night shivering in bed awaiting her return. When she tried to give me the slip a few nights later, I followed her out the door.

Jasmine's newly acquired boyfriend, Kebir, was waiting for her on the other side of the street. He wore a greasy leather jacket and looked mean and unwanted. Rather than stay alone in the room, I spent the next few nights following them through the streets and bars and back alleys of the town, always fearful that I'd lose sight of them. Except for an occasional burst of recognition, in which he'd order me a Coke or crack an unpleasant smile, Kebir ignored me. Eventually I'd clear a space for myself on the table, lower my head, and fall asleep. I was getting good at sleeping on tables.

The roof of the hotel was inhabited by the tourists. They spent the day sunning themselves, smoking cigarettes and drinking coffee. One day, as I was leaning over the side, I saw a man stride purposefully down the street. I noticed him because, unlike the aimless crowds around him, his walk was deliberate, confident. He wore a shirt with a collar and beige pants; no brightly patterned clothes, no sunglasses. As I watched, transfixed, the man's face come into focus. It was my father.

"Daddy!" I shouted. "Up here!"

He turned his face up towards me and waved.

I wasn't on the roof long enough to wave back. I bounded down the stairs to the street and threw myself into his arms.

"Look at you," my father said. "A young Lawrence of Arabia."

Although I was overjoyed at the thought of liberation from the hotel, I was puzzled about my father's casual arrival. This was a man who could park his car on a street corner and spend the next four hours trying to find it.

He asked me where my mother was.

"I don't know," I answered.

"I suspect she'll show up soon."

My mother's vanishing act was her way of being discovered: my father could render her in vivid colours only when she removed herself from the sitter's stool. And my father could always sense the moment when my mother might break away. That was when he would come and claim her. He had left Italy and flown to England, picked up her scent, and followed it all the way down the coast of Morocco.

He'd come to take away my mother's independence — or rather her pretense of independence. He did so by offering another pretense: that of his own dependence upon her. His absent-mindedness, his profound lack of interest in domestic affairs — a lack of interest so profound it bordered on infidelity — all were part of his claim of dependence. It was my mother who placed the stamps on letters. It was she who dropped them off at the corner postbox. The movement of paper and plates, the arrival and removal of guests, all were tinged with magic in my father's eyes. He took an almost childlike delight at the sight of a letter popping through a mail slot, of a roast being taken out of the oven.

And so his accomplished arrival that day in the small Moroccan town of Essaouira was all the more mysterious to me. His trek across the desert signified an ability to consult train timetables, calculate distances, and prepare for border formalities. He had procured a fashionable hotel room overlooking the sea, a room we shared while waiting for my mother. His assurance that I would eat well, his unspoken promise not to leave my side day or night was more than unusual. It was peculiar. This man, my father, was actually looking after me. He had taken me out of the hotel with dispatch and, for the first time, established order in my life. He had actually tailored his mood to better my own.

My mother appeared a few days later, just as he'd said she would. Neither showed any surprise at the other's arrival, nor did they exhibit any sense of wariness. They simply dismantled their recently acquired armour and placed the pieces in their respective corners, ready for future combat.

An audience soon formed around my father, procured in part by Nada, who let it be known among the roof tourists and others that a great poet was in their midst. Relaxed and masterful as if he were sitting in his own living room, my father spoke to young men and women about the need for poetry and the necessity of desire. My mother hovered in the background. Her brief moment in the sun had come to an end.

Chapter 2

FAULT LINES

M y mother kept insisting we move to Forest Hill, Forest Hill being where respectable people lived. That was my mother's opinion anyway, and she wouldn't stop until all of us were safely ensconced in one of its solid brick houses. At first my father resisted what he diagnosed as "house-mania," but my mother was adamant. She wished to be respectable and that was that.

As long as there was food on the table and an attic to work in, my father couldn't have cared less where he lived. Being oblivious to his family meant he could readily ignore his neighbours. But moving to Forest Hill meant money.

"We *have* money, Irving," was my mother's constant reply to any of my father's financial hesitations.

"In the other world we'll have money. In this one we're poor."

"But I hate this house. It's mean and everything is falling apart."

This was true. An inspector had come to examine our house several weeks before and had pointed to a crack between the wall and the chimney. He called it a "fault line."

The line was hard to locate at first, but if we followed the inspector's pointed finger carefully with our eyes, we could see clear through to the neighbour's house. My mother was horrified.

We followed the chimney up to the second floor. This time, when my mother looked through the crack, she could see the sky, the rooftops, the ground beneath her feet.

The "cloven house," as my mother put it, had to be abandoned. Never one to turn down a usable symbol, she proclaimed that this house represented everything that was unstable, broken, rotten. With life, as with the house, it was only a matter of knowing where to look.

My mother's perfect house sat on Delavan Avenue, a small side street on the southern fringes of Forest Hill. The house was fully detached, solid, and, compared with some of the other houses in the area, relatively modest.

A woman met us at the door. Her face was so sharp she could have sliced a piece of paper with it, and her makeup didn't help either. The swirls of colour on her face made me think of rotten fruit.

My mother and the woman moved immediately towards the kitchen and answered each other's questions, occasionally referring to a sheet of paper that rested on the kitchen counter. The exchange of information was brief, organized, and strangely intense, as if they were sharing a secret.

"Well, why don't you look around?" the woman said, smiling. Surprisingly, this statement was addressed to me.

My mother led me upstairs and as we walked into

"my bedroom," it became apparent she'd been through this house before. She pointed to the sliding door. "This will give you lots of light," she said. The sliding door led out to a bare roof covered with grey pebbles. There were no guardrails.

We entered the bathroom, we peered into a closet, then we walked into what my mother called the "master bedroom." This was a new expression, one I'd never heard her use before. I suspected that the word was lifted from the sheet of paper she'd taken off the kitchen counter and which I now held in my hand. The front page was littered with words, the ink deep and black. The back page contained several diagrams. There, in small letters, inside a rectangular box, were the words I was looking for — "Master B.R."

My mother stooped down and rubbed her hand against the plush beige carpet.

"Take your shoes off," she commanded.

I began to back out of the room.

"Look at this. You can sink your toes into the carpet."

I had a sudden urge to run out of the house.

I found myself at the foot of another staircase, narrower than the first, which led to the attic. These were familiar steps — I knew where they led to and I knew who would be using them. On my way up the stairs, I heard my mother's voice call out from below.

"Isn't it wonderful?"

Every house I had ever lived in had steps leading to a third floor, and every third floor resembled this one. The front window looked out over the street; it was the view my father would enjoy while sitting at his desk. I moved towards the back of the room where the sloping roof formed a small alcove. This cramped space would house my father's steel cabinets. I could even detect the future aroma which my father's labour would deposit in the room.

My mother had followed me up the stairs and insisted on pointing out the various features that appealed to her. The windows, she said, were double-glazed.

"But they can still be opened for summer," she added. It was clear that only one person was meant to benefit from this open window and he wasn't here. The third-floor attic had always been the most secretive part of the house, the one I was least familiar with. Strangely, it was now the only room I could imagine occupied. Even in his absence, my father was solid enough to command a room of his own.

"Well, how do you like the house?" my mother asked.

I moved towards the centre of the room. One last survey of my surroundings, and then I proclaimed the words my mother had been waiting for. "I love it!"

Her cheeks, already flushed with delight, turned an even fiercer red.

Forest Hill Village was only a short walk away and my mother wanted to show me its many "advantages," chief among them being that it was a village.

"It's just like Europe," she kept repeating. We were now walking along the edge of a narrow park. A sign offered a clarification; it was a "parkette."

To help authenticate her village story, my mother told me that the area in which we now found ourselves had once really been a small village, independent and completely separate from the rest of the city. It was only later

— much later — she assured me, that it had been swallowed up. The very thought of it made her indignant.

Apparently, Forest Hill was engaged in a silent war with the city which now surrounded it. Once my mother pointed this out to me, it was easy to recognize the battle-fields. The lawns of Forest Hill weren't the rectangular patches studded with dog shit and squirrel holes that I was used to. These garden patches were terraced with stones, shaped and sculptured. And there weren't any dogs, unleashed and alone, roaming the neighbourhood, just parked cars, silent and obedient.

"Well, here we are."

My mother stood outside a grocery store; when she opened the door a bell jangled above her head. A thin layer of sawdust was sprinkled over the floorboards; it was similar in colour to the beige carpet my mother had been so eager for me to stick my bare toes into.

The shelves were full but not crowded, and reached all the way to the ceiling. Several fans, their fins painted green, spun slowly around. Behind a glass counter lay thick slices of meat and plump yellow chickens, gar-nished with plastic parsley. A black woman stood behind the counter holding a steak that drooped over the edges of her hand. A slice of waxed paper separated her hand from the meat, which she slid off and placed on a metal scale. A customer nodded in approval, then silently waited for her meat to be wrapped in a brown sheet of waxed paper.

It became clear to me that my mother had no intention of purchasing anything from the store, and I was relieved when we crossed the street to the local pharmacy.

"First time here?" the white-coated man behind the counter asked, after my mother placed several items on the counter.

"Yes, it is."

"Have you just moved into the area?"

"Actually, I've just come from looking at a house on Delavan."

"That's a lovely street," he said, returning my mother's change.

My mother agreed with the man in the white coat. Then she took her bottles and walked out the front door.

"Do you see how friendly everyone is here!" My mother's pupils, which had been increasing in diameter throughout the day, were now fully dilated. We were standing on the sidewalk, just outside the pharmacy.

"Everyone knows who you are. It's just like a real place."

I found this last statement rather disturbing. If my mother could become excited about a place simply because it was real, then it must be because she felt our present household was unreal. I had to admit that I'd been vaguely aware of this fact for some time. There was nothing vague about my mother's feelings, though. She'd known all along.

Her present enthusiasm had been ignited by the man in the white coat, whom my mother referred to as a "chemist," yet another word she'd never used before, at least not in my presence. I began to wonder if Forest Hill required a different vocabulary from the one I'd become accustomed to.

Although I'd barely listened to their conversation, it hadn't seemed much different from countless others my mother had engaged in over the years. And yet she had made it clear that this man possessed certain qualities not found anywhere else.

I couldn't imagine why, since he suffered from what my father called "the receding forest"; all that remained of his hair was a slim line on the edge of his neck. Through my father, I had come to associate baldness with a lack of moral vigour, the result of small fears accumulated over time.

Personally, I found the "village" a severe disappointment. The stores seemed not so different from those my mother wished to leave behind, and the people who inhabited them were merely strangers, rather than the exotics my mother claimed them to be.

But she was insistent that these people belonged to a different world, a better world. One that would make her real.

A week after the inspector's visit to our old house, my mother had her wisdom teeth yanked out. When she returned from the dentist she sank onto the bed, crossed her legs, and began to chant "*Om mane padme hum.*" The house filled up with unhappy sounds.

My mother's refusal to open her bruised eyes provoked a deep commitment in me to torment her.

The crack was clearly visible from my mother's bed. I'd stand in front of the wall and comment on the wondrous sights that lay beyond. "The birds are swarming!" I'd say. I was enthralled by my own malice. Yet for all the strength it gave me, I never managed to make my mother open her eyes. Her stubbornness was clearly superior to my own.

My father became worried.

"My beautiful raccoon," he'd say, referring to her blackened eyes. My mother's assigned nickname was a sure sign he was nervous. I couldn't help noticing that, as an overall strategy, his use of nicknames was a spectacular failure. It often provoked hysteria which, I began to see, might have been the point all along.

"My wonderful little raccoon." When desperate, he even tried to tickle her chin.

Since my mother wouldn't open her eyes for him either, my father took to sitting alone at the dining-room table, glumly chewing the cold food he'd pulled out of the refrigerator. I'd sit on the living-room floor, playing with my toy planes; a silent idle to the runway, then a slow steady ascent.

Upstairs, from the bedroom, my mother's sad wail continued unabated.

"*Om mane padme hum.*"

And she didn't open her eyes until a "For Sale" sign was pitched on the front lawn.

Our first move was to an apartment building overlooking Forest Hill Village. According to my mother, this temporary move was caused by "timing." Our old house was sold before we'd managed to buy the other one. Apparently, we'd been sitting on a double lot, which meant that the cloven house could be knocked down and replaced with two new ones.

"They're going to put up townhouses," my mother sniffed disdainfully. I got the impression that the neighbourhood we had lived in for the last two years deserved this ugly blemish, a retaliatory measure for not having given her the house of her dreams.

The double-lot discovery had been somewhat miraculous, a possible and positive sign that the gods approved of our move to Forest Hill. The house had been sold and, as my mother was fond of pointing out, it had been sold at a fair profit.

"Any more profit and we'll be bankrupt," was my father's gloomy reply.

The sale was conditional on our immediate evacuation, as the buyers wished to have it demolished as quickly as possible, an aspiration fully shared by my mother.

The building we now lived in was guarded by a doorman who was my father's age. Grey-haired and uniformed, he wore a long overcoat with Christmas ornaments attached to the sleeves and shoulders.

My father had a fear of idle men, and the doorman, despite his upright bearing, seemed supremely idle. He opened doors and the doors closed by themselves. His job was so preposterous I felt certain he'd been employed for darker reasons.

The doorman gave my father the same shallow nod he reserved for everyone else who walked through his doors. Over the years, I'd become accustomed to people, often complete strangers, acknowledging my father's presence. They'd stop him on the street or interrupt his meal. Most wished simply to shake his hand; a few informed him that he'd changed their lives. No matter what the reason, my father always managed to match their enthusiasm with his own, proffering advice when asked, or signing books.

"You see that, my boy? Your father is famous!" he'd say, slapping my arm.

He exhibited an equal, though far less frequent, enthusiasm for avoiding these encounters.

"My God, let's cross the street. All that man wants to do is talk about poetry."

If caught, he couldn't contain himself. I'd stand beside him for twenty minutes, patiently waiting for the conversation about poetry to come to an end.

That's why I was unused to the doorman's response

to my father; he lacked enthusiasm. My father, who was perfectly capable of flirting with sixty-year-old Hungarian waitresses, or informing young men that they carried the divine spirit of Zeus within their bellies, was equally tepid.

I felt sorry for the doorman for not knowing who my father was. And I felt sorry for my father who seemed incapable of telling him. It was an unpleasant daily encounter, one which I tried to avoid.

Unable to escape to the attic, my father banged up against the thin walls of the apartment. He could not be adequately contained, although my mother did her best by keeping the doors to every room tightly shut. Still, he needed only breathe, as my mother pointed out, for his presence to be known. Wherever I was — in the living room, my own room, even the toilet — my father's presence became oppressive. He was always on the other side, breathing. I imagined that the moisture which leaked from his nose would dissolve the walls around him. Even then he would not be able to escape — his entrapment would become our own.

My father grew restless once he picked up the scent of food, and I'd hear his chair scrape against the floor as he lifted himself up. He often moved out to the balcony, where he'd squeeze into another chair and stare at the metal railing until dinner was ready.

One day my grandmother, my mother's mother, joined him on the balcony. My mother must have brought her over from Australia on the assumption that we'd all be safely tucked behind the solid walls of the new house, but her timing was off. Now that we had one more body in need of privacy, my grandmother absorbed what limited space we had left.

I only had one grandparent. The rest, apparently, were all dead, although I never felt entirely sure about this. My father had seven brothers and sisters and I'd never met any of them. A few were dead, the rest were missing.

Even though I knew my other grandmother was dead, she still seemed accessible. My father always spoke of her "presence." He had two stories about those who looked on from afar, the stories contradictory. The first person was God. As a young boy, my father had turned on the light in defiance of Sabbath rules. He fully expected to be hit with a bolt of lightning so, when God's power failed to exert itself, he decided that God wasn't merely impotent, He was imaginary.

Not so his mother. Once, while driving on a dirt road at night in the hills of Greece, my father had lost control of his car and it veered towards the cliff. It was his mother who had placed her hand on the car's hood and prevented it from plummeting off the edge.

Apart from the ghost of his dead mother, my father showed no interest in the supernatural. I often waited for him to dismiss other people's accounts of ghosts and gods but he rarely bothered, preferring instead to confront these stories with glazed eyes. The one time I saw him play the Ouija board, his stubby finger brought the pointer to a complete standstill.

"It appears no one wishes to speak to me," he complained.

This was not quite true. The thirteen-year-old girl whose spirit we had raised and whose premature death by drowning had reduced my mother to tears was of no interest to someone like my father. He had other ways of speaking to the dead.

Feeling skeptical about the supernatural myself, I should have felt disappointed in my father's belief in his mother's ghost. Instead, I felt jealousy. Her presence was clearly defined, well established, documented, and powerful. From Montreal to the hills of Greece, my paternal grandmother's reach was extensive. Surely such a woman, if she was interested, could have made herself known to me. Yet it seemed that she had eyes only for her son.

After much persistence I'd been given a set of hockey pads, a face mask, a blocker, and a glove to catch the pucks thrown against me every Saturday at the Eglinton hockey arena. I belonged to a team called Coal Port China, a name which remained forever mysterious to me, and attempted to block shots against teams named after restaurants and hardware stores. Coal Port China, perhaps lacking a recognizable sponsor, offered inadequate equipment for the task at hand and I'd wailed to my mother about the oversized hockey pads I was forced to wear each weekend and about how, as my coach said, I couldn't "eat the puck" with enough enthusiasm. I wasn't "hungry" enough. I needed better protection. I wanted my own equipment.

My mother had held off buying me anything until our move to Forest Hill, perhaps sensing that only here in this magical village could any serious attempt be made to eliminate family needs. The problem was I no longer belonged to a hockey arena, Eglinton being too far away. I did have brand-new equipment, though, which I strapped onto my body each evening. Fully armoured and behind closed doors, I'd throw yellow tennis balls against the wall and hurl myself at the rebounds.

I was caked in sweat when my mother called me out for dinner one evening, a summons I ignored. She wasn't alone. My half-brother, Max, was in the living room with Stephanie, his new girlfriend. They were joined shortly afterwards by my father and Leonard, who'd been taking a walk through the neighbourhood. I heard my father proclaim that they'd been out "hunting ideas," which made me wonder, as I threw tennis balls against the wall, what rich game existed within the confines of Forest Hill.

My mother called me out for dinner again and I told her to fuck off.

"David!" my mother cried. She made the mistake of opening the door. I threw her out of my room and pinned her against the living-room wall, my arms around her waist, my face mask pushed against her belly.

"David!" she wailed. "We have guests!"

As I turned away from my mother's belly, I could see them through the two peepholes of my hockey mask. They were sitting around the dining-room table, my father and Leonard at either end. I agreed to join them, but only if I could wear my hockey equipment. Shuffling over in my hockey pads, I sat beside Max.

Wishing to inject a sense of normalcy, my mother asked Stephanie if she preferred white or dark meat.

"That all depends, Aviva," she answered slyly.

"On what?" my father demanded, but before Stephanie could answer, Leonard asked her what she did.

"I'm a waitress."

"But you must be more than that."

"I'm an artist."

"Where do you work?"

"At the top of the Toronto-Dominion Tower."

"What time do you get off? I'd like to come and visit."

"Hey, Leonard!" my brother shouted. "Stop trying to pick up my girlfriend."

My father started to laugh: "You have to watch out for him, son."

Stephanie turned towards my father and pointed to the large medallion which hung around his neck.

"Do you know what that is?" she asked him.

"What?" my father asked, suddenly annoyed.

"Do you know what that is hanging around your neck?"

My father briefly glanced down at his silver medallion and became angered that he'd been made to do so.

"Yes, yes," he said dismissively, but Stephanie ignored him.

"It's the hand of Fatima. The symbol of protection. Do you know why?"

"What!" my father shouted again. Her challenge made his face puff with anger.

"Fatima was Muhammad's daughter. One day she heard that her beloved husband, Ali, was leaving for a holy war and in despair she asked to go with him, to offer protection, but Ali said this was impossible, because a woman couldn't go to war. So Fatima dipped her hand in henna and placed it over Ali's heart, leaving an imprint which couldn't be washed off. She believed that even at a distance the power of her love could protect him."

My father said nothing, burying his face in the plate of food my mother put in front of him. Embarrassed by his silence, my mother turned to Leonard and said, "Oh look, what's that around *your* neck?"

Leonard looked up at my mother: "It's an albatross, Aviva."

My grandmother and I went for a walk to the village. I carried a droopy straw bag that my grandmother had found in one of the cupboards. The coarse material, embellished with faded strips of embroidery, clearly identified the bag as Moroccan.

"Small pieces of the past," was what my mother called the dozens of trinkets she'd brought back from her travels.

I was embarrassed to carry the bag, which was clearly out of place in Forest Hill; I suspected it was out of place in Morocco too.

Unlike my mother, whose desire to save the environment came in such sudden noisy bursts that I suspected her hatred of plastic bags was based on a fear she'd use one to suffocate my father, my grandmother's decision to use the Moroccan bag was based on simple frugality.

"Your parents love you very much, David," she said gently as we began the descent into the village. As I hadn't asked for an opinion either way, I remained silent.

"It's just that adults sometimes act like children themselves."

I thought about this. If adults could sometimes act like children, then surely children could sometimes act like adults, a fact which perhaps explained the tender but direct fashion my grandmother now used when speaking to me.

"My parents are idiots!" I shouted.

My grandmother smiled, but said nothing more. It was clear I'd gone too far.

That evening, as my mother made supper with the supplies handed to her in the Moroccan bag, I noticed for the first time that my father was closer in age to my grandmother than to the woman cooking his food.

They sat on two chairs facing each other, my father

and my grandmother, feet on the floor, backs nestled into cushions. I couldn't help noticing how closely the posture of their bodies matched the tone of their voices. They appeared eminently sensible, relaxed, and civilized.

The sound of clashing pots momentarily diverted my attention towards the kitchen, but the noise failed to elicit even a faint response from the two elders in the living room, who carried on with their discussion as if nothing had happened. I'd thought there were only two people engaged in the conversation, but with my mother noisily returning the pots to their shelves I realized that I was mistaken — there were three.

That night my grandmother came to tuck me in. She sat on the side of my bed and began to sing, gently stroking my arm from shoulder to elbow. I was now a child; in the afternoon, I had been an adult. This shift was at my grandmother's discretion, but even a woman as solid as my grandmother had become entangled in the changing alliances of the household. This afternoon both my parents had been children; later that night it was just my mother who had banged pots in the kitchen for attention. Perhaps tomorrow it would be my father.

My new school was only a short walk away. Forest Hill Junior High had a Coke machine, which greatly impressed me, and a small tuck shop, which impressed me even more. I could buy french fries and Oh Henry! bars with abandon.

My first day was spent in what was called a home-room. It was here — so Mr. Bunt, our homeroom teacher, said — that we would assemble each morning before heading off to our various classes.

Several months later, in my English class, I would

be formally introduced to the literary term "foreshadow-
ing," but Mr. Bunt was courteous enough to give me an
early lesson on my very first day of school.

After informing us of the various rules and regu-
lations, he told the class that he had a special announcement to make. There was among us, he said, the son of a
great poet.

"Does anyone know what a poet does?" Mr. Bunt
asked. I had to admit that I was interested in the answer
myself, but nobody raised a hand.

Mr. Bunt assumed this was due to first-day shyness,
rather than stupidity.

"Anyone? C'mon, I'm sure someone in this class
knows what a poet does." He turned his kind face to me
and smiled. Obviously he thought I knew, but it was
important for both of us to refrain from answering. Let
others shine.

"They write poems," a girl answered.

"Exactly," said Mr. Bunt. "And what is a poem?"

"It's when you rhyme words."

"That's right. And your name is?" he asked.

"Suki," she replied. Suki's layered hair was better
managed than my mother's.

"Suki, do all poems have to rhyme?"

"I don't think so," she said.

"David, what do you think?"

I was shocked that he knew my name. Up till then
I had held out hope that there was another student in the
class whose father was a poet.

"No," was all I could say.

"No," repeated Mr. Bunt, amplifying my answer,
"David's right. Poems don't have to rhyme. In fact the very
best ones usually don't, but that doesn't mean they don't
have rhythm."

I nodded conspiratorially.

There was a moment of silence, before I heard my name being called again. Unfortunately Mr. Bunt was having a conversation with me and I was now expected to answer. Rhythm, I thought? What the fuck is he talking about?

"What's your father's name?" This question came from Lawrence Weinstein, a plump student with a name tag stuck to his orange turtleneck sweater.

"Irving Layton," I answered. My father's name sounded ridiculous.

"Does anyone know the name of any other Canadian poets?"

There was complete silence.

"Leonard Cohen? Has anyone heard of Leonard Cohen?" Mr. Bunt, ever thoughtful, wished to stimulate our memories.

No one raised their hands.

"He's also a singer," Mr. Bunt added, again looking in my direction. This time I thought I could see a shadow of doubt in his smile.

"You look like David Cassidy." This too was from Weinstein, who pointed a finger in my direction. The link between my face and that of David Cassidy's had been made years before by a group of girls in my Grade Three class. Back then, it was meant as a compliment. Now it could only mean certain disaster. I looked at Suki and knew it was time for a haircut.

My first friend at school was Juan. He was a Chilean refugee who would jump into the bushes whenever he spotted a man in uniform. Nobody liked him. I didn't

like him. His olive skin exuded sweat and moisture collected above his upper lip, which was darker than the rest
of him; it gave him the appearance of wearing a weedy
moustache. To make matters worse, Juan wore oversized
red-framed glasses. The powerful lenses dimmed the
light in his eyes and made him appear permanently
stunned.

Juan's first jump into the bushes took me by surprise, but I soon became accustomed to his evasive action.
I would jump into the bush after him, grab his shaking
body, and berate him for his stupidity.

"It's only a postman."

As with my mother and her cracked wall, I was
moved not by a sense of compassion, but by its opposite:
I had a deep desire to torment Juan, and he made a beautiful victim.

When I told my mother about my new friend, she
became concerned. In her attempt to explain the peculiarities of Juan's native country, she referred to Greece
where, as she explained, a group of men – a "junta," she
called it – controlled the country, much to the annoyance
of other people, people like Juan and his family.

"Junta" – I loved the sound of that word; it made
Juan more exciting to me. My memories of Greece were
all pleasant. More than pleasant, they were glorious. If
Juan came from such a place, he was lucky.

Despite such thoughts, my mother's concern had
an effect on me. My passion for tormenting Juan was
improper, and I felt ashamed.

Juan was the only student whose skin colour was
darker than the linoleum floor beneath our feet, but the
skin of Mr. Mitchell, our math and English teacher, was
far darker.

Mr. Mitchell was Jamaican. His hands were broad

but elegant, his long fingers tipped with ivory-coloured fingernails. He often wore a suit and tie; on days when his dress was more casual, his tie-less shirt reminded me of a tablecloth without its cutlery.

Mr. Mitchell was a strict disciplinarian and the school placed two types of students in his class: those who excelled and those who didn't. I had no doubt to which category I belonged and, with time, neither did Mr. Bunt, who had mercifully stopped asking me to explain poetry to the class; in fact, he'd stopped asking me to explain anything.

Mr. Mitchell had strict requirements, one of them being that he admitted only one type of ruler into his classroom. It was to be fifteen inches — what he called "regulation size" — and preferably made of wood. Nothing else would do, and I was forever running up and down hallways anxiously searching for rulers to borrow. Soon even the generous at heart were fatigued by my constant demands and began to withhold their regulation rulers from my prying hands. I found it inexplicable that I chose to live with such constant anxiety, when it could have been so easily remedied. What the hell was wrong with me? With each new feverish search, I promised myself I would never be without a ruler. But it wasn't long before I came to the class empty-handed yet again.

"What's this?" Mr. Mitchell asked.

"What's what?" I answered.

This was not the kind of response Mr. Mitchell had patience for. He began to move towards me and the cracked plastic ruler which I'd tried to conceal beneath my math book.

"I've lost mine," I whined.

Mr. Mitchell planted both his hands on the edge of my desk and leaned over.

"Kid, you're a damn baby-boy."

His face was so close to mine, I could feel the hot breath blow out of his mouth.

"She has green apples."

This was Juan's description of Roberta's breasts. I found his assessment deeply unsettling. The two small bumps beneath Roberta's shirt were an overwhelming concern of mine, and Juan, whose position in the class afforded an unobstructed view, became an expert on their shape and size. In his estimation, Roberta's breasts were unripened apples, sour and hard. I had recently recovered from a minor chest infection which had coalesced around my left nipple, hardening the surrounding skin and making it sore to the touch. I imagined that Roberta's breasts were somehow equally inflamed and sore, a kind of infection.

Only two things disrupted Juan's passivity in the classroom: Mr. Mitchell's accusatory finger and Roberta's breasts. As far as I knew, the fascination with Roberta's breasts wasn't shared by anyone except Juan and myself, but when Mr. Mitchell used the word "come" in his conversation – a not infrequent occurrence – a furtive excitement flushed our faces. Weinstein was usually the instigator. He'd roll his eyes for a few seconds, before dropping them to his crotch.

For a man who observed even the slightest infraction in his classroom, Mr. Mitchell was as oblivious to Weinstein's whirling eyeballs as he was to the word that set them in motion. This was due in part to Mr. Mitchell's desire to arouse in us an appreciation of language, quite different from the one he was now inadvertently causing.

Mr. Mitchell was engrossed in the book *Shane*, copies of which, in various forms of decay, sat on each of our desks. The book was a Western which, Mr. Mitchell made clear, enabled it to be classified as a "genre," a word I found imposing and therefore wholly unsuitable for the book which now lay in front of me.

The book's dull cloth cover was made even duller by the numerous hands which had touched it in the past. The names of these past owners were written in pencil (an HB lead tip, the only kind Mr. Mitchell approved of) on the inside back cover. Each previous name had a line drawn through it, and made my own name, which I'd recently pencilled in beneath the others, seem impermanent.

I wondered if each owner was responsible for his own eventual erasure or if it was the responsibility of Mr. Mitchell. As yet my name remained unharmed.

With a copy of the book resting on the open palm of his right hand, Mr. Mitchell expounded to the class about the merits and glories of *Shane*. He marvelled at its construction, pointing out how the economy of words used throughout the book corresponded to its laconic hero, a man who, he pointed out, never sat with his back exposed.

Despite Mr. Mitchell's best efforts, I found the book a disappointment. The prying eyes of all those previous owners had somehow taken the life out of it. The insights of Mr. Mitchell had been repeated before, many times, year after year, and it made his remarks appear stale and deeply unoriginal.

But it was more than that; I was disappointed in Mr. Mitchell for choosing such a book. My father had a large collection of books in his study, many of which spilled out into the rest of the household. They were old, many of them wrapped in a cloth that had faded to an even duller shade of brown than my copy of *Shane*. But that was where the similarities ended. My father's books seemed important, vibrant. An Olympian runner, a torch in his hand, was often embossed on the spine. My mother had once told me a story about a Greek runner who'd been entrusted with an important message. He had run all day and all night and when he reached Athens, he delivered his message and died. I was certain that the runner in my mother's story was the same runner who graced my father's books. Alone in his study, I'd pull a book out of its bookcase and smell it.

Sometimes I'd come across other names in my father's books. A few even had sentences penned by a different hand. These were never crossed out; they remained in the book, untouched and insignificant beside my father's signature and date.

All I could make out of my father's signature was the letter "I" for Irving and the letter "L" for Layton. The rest was a blur, a cryptic scribble. For some reason I thought that my own signature would be similar to my father's, but it wasn't. My own name, legible and obvious, was written with a weak hand, soon to be crossed out like the rest of them and replaced by another name.

My father wouldn't have touched a book like *Shane*, and I was surprised that Mr. Mitchell found the book worthy of his attention. Its hero inhabited a different and, I felt, inferior world, a desolate place where no one spoke except when necessary.

Mr. Mitchell, on the other hand, had another life, one which was revealed through his admonishments.

"Kid, I used to walk five damn miles to school and five damn miles back," he'd say to those who arrived late to class.

He mentioned something about tree stumps for

chairs, wild rivers, and rainstorms, but it was a world far too exotic to be fully comprehensible under the fluorescent lights of our overheated classroom. After school, we'd laugh at Mr. Mitchell's hardships, which seemed too harsh to be true. It was impossible that such a man would arrive here in Forest Hill, and be able to speak our language. But inside his classroom no one laughed, and when Mr. Mitchell said he walked five damn miles to school we all knew that he'd walked those five damn miles.

My encounter with Jamaicans didn't end with Mr. Mitchell's class. We had now moved into our new house and my mother was bent on reducing its innards to a pile of rubble. Things, she said, needed to be changed — transformed — and four Jamaican men were there to help in this endeavour. They ripped out toilets and bathtubs, tore down ceilings, reduced kitchen cabinets to splintered wood. Every day when I returned from school, there was another area of the house smashed and destroyed. The accumulation of debris over the days was devastating; soon we were swinging down a rope to the basement in order to take a pee, the rest of the bathrooms and the staircase to the basement having been destroyed days before.

The four Jamaicans, who carried a portable radio with a silver grille, had extraordinary destructive abilities. It was construction that became problematic. Days went by, and then weeks, before new cabinets were fitted for the kitchen. My mother complained the doors were crooked.

I was quickly dissuaded from the notion that my mother had some master plan for putting things back together again. She would roam the house, confusion clouding her face. Neither my father nor I could understand why she wanted to rip down a perfectly good house, and after a while it became clear my mother didn't know either.

"I paid good money for that," my father would say as the American Standard toilet was being carried out, but my mother didn't listen to him and neither did the Jamaicans. They threw it onto the front lawn and eventually a truck came and took it away.

One day the ceiling fell down. I came back from school and found my mother sitting on the sofa, pounds of white plaster scattered about her. The Jamaicans were nowhere to be found, but I'd seen them on ladders the day before, smoothing out the lines and bubbles of the wet plaster with their metal tools. When I looked up at the ceiling, I noticed that there wasn't much left to smooth out.

My mother just sat there on the sofa, too tired to cry, staring in my direction but unable to acknowledge my presence. It took me a while to realize that my father was in the kitchen, pouring a glass of water for her. Normally, in moments of crisis, my father would disappear to the attic — his study was the only room which had remained untouched — but now he was here, on the same floor, handing my mother the water and placing his hand on her shoulder.

"It'll be all right, Aviva," he said. It took his gentle gesture to make me realize the seriousness of my mother's condition.

The next morning a taxi pulled up to the house and took my mother away. Her packed suitcase had been sitting in the hallway since the previous night. I kissed her goodbye and watched my father place her bag in the car, then help her into the taxi.

"She's gone to a hotel for a few nights," he said, returning to the front door. We had our breakfast and then went our separate ways.

During the course of the next several days, a new set of workmen went about fixing the house. Although my father was nowhere in sight, the men worked with purpose and design and, when my mother returned to the house, she no longer had to swing down a rope to take a pee.

I wanted a dog. My mother and I went to the pet store and, for $350, purchased a Pomeranian no taller than the length of my foot. The people at P.J. Pets assured both my mother and me that it was a reasonable price for a pure-bred dog with all its shots.

We had obtained another dog from the pound a few weeks earlier which promptly dove under the couch and refused to come out, snapping at our outstretched hands and snarling at the bowls of food we laid out. My mother thought he was rabid. Emerging once from his lair, he had run madly along the edge of the walls until he'd come full circle, then dove back under the couch, more violent and paranoid than before.

Two men from the pound came to get him the next day. They were what my father would call "burly," with tattoos on their forearms and heavy boots on their feet. They looked like members of a motorcycle gang. One of the men crouched down and called out to the dog in a voice that was surprisingly tender. Within a short time the dog was rubbing the tip of his snout against the man's out-stretched fingers.

"He's a good dog," the man said. It was a statement of fact rather than an apology, and it was clear from the tone of his voice that he believed we had something to do with the dog's psychotic behaviour.

Our purebred Pomeranian yapped ferociously in the back of the car as we made our way back to the house. Her tail shot straight up, then curled inward. This was a permanent condition — a Pomeranian "feature." We called her Foxy Lady.

Foxy Lady was our sentinel at 33 Delavan Avenue, a dog so high-strung that her reaction to our household was, unlike the other dog's, negligible. Since she had begun her life as an hysteric, she felt right at home.

When winter arrived, I'd throw her out the front door into a deep pile of snow. Her initial struggle helped sink her like a stone, the deep snow walls crumbling with every shake of her paw. I'd wait for defeat to overtake her, a silent wet animal shivering in the cold, then leap from the front steps and rescue her, wrapping my arms tightly around her body.

"Foxy, you shouldn't get stuck in the snow," I'd say, taking her into the house to dry. Stunned by her recent mishap, Foxy Lady would remain beside me for a few minutes, but as soon as her tail popped back up she'd struggle to free herself from my embracing arms.

"Foxy, come back here. I need to warm you up," I'd say, mimicking the burly man's tone of voice. My voice was sweeter than his, more sinister; my intent was unclean.

Her refusal to accept my charity sent me into a rage.

"You little bitch, come back here."

I chased her around the house and when I got close enough I tried to kick her in the ass.

I was hanging on to my mother's leg, both arms wrapped firmly around her ankle. She was trying to dislodge me, shaking her leg while dragging me across the dining-room floor. "David, you have to stop this!"

"No! No! No!" I slid along the floor on my belly, kicking my feet as if I were swimming in the ocean.

"David," she said, bending down to pat my head, "you have to stop this."

"Fuck you!"

"Let go of me."

I wouldn't.

I was dragged into the kitchen, where my mother developed a new strategy; she pretended I wasn't on the ground, clenched to her leg. She dragged me to the left, picked out a pot, then dragged me to the right and placed the pot on the stove. When she went to open the fridge door, I stuck out my head.

"You hit me!" I screamed.

My mother began to hum a tune.

"You don't care," I added. I went into convulsions on the kitchen floor, failing to stop until my mother acknowledged my presence.

"Stop it!" she screamed.

"No!"

"Go do your homework." This request was made only in times of crisis and was used as a form of punishment. I began to shake more violently.

"You don't want to be a moron, do you?"

I let go of her foot and raced down the hallway.

"Moron!" she yelled. "Idiot!"

Now it was my mother who was shaking violently, sobbing into her pot.

"I don't know what to do with you."

Her despair was soothing, like the Vicks Vaporub

she rubbed on my chest when I had a cold. I felt a momentary flush of heat, then I was able to breathe.

"Your father will have to say something."

I was unsure if this was meant as a threat to me or to my father, but during the evening when I was supposed to be in bed, I placed myself at the top of the stairs and watched my parents in the living room. It wasn't long before my mother caught me perched over the wooden banister, staring down at the top of her head.

"Go to bed," she ordered.

I waited, silent, implacable, thinking myself a stone gargoyle. I tried not to breathe.

"Irving, say something."

My father sat in his chair, book in hand, another implacable gargoyle she was forced to live with.

"Irving!"

"Hurrrr," he grunted, not taking his eyes off the book.

His voice was enough to send me scurrying to my room, but the effect wore off before I reached the door. I came back and returned to my stoic endeavour.

"Irving, you have to discipline your child," my mother pleaded. Her voice was muted but clearly audible; it lent her a conspiratorial air.

"Hurrrr," he grunted again, this time waving his right arm in the air. I wasn't sure if this was meant for me or for my mother. Halfway to my door, I heard him finish with a "Burrah." These peculiar sounds, foreign and impressive, came from the depths of my father's belly, but they held no more importance than letting out air; his noises were merely signs of mild indigestion.

Upon my return to the top of the stairs my mother, in desperation, began to lecture my father.

"I can't always be the one to tell David what to do. You have to take on some responsibility too."

Finally, my father put his book down, rose to his feet, and shouted, "Go to bed!" Then he stamped his feet.

My mother followed me back to my bedroom. Pulling the covers over me, she sat down on the side of the bed.

"Why do we always fight?" I asked my mother.

"I don't know, but let's not do it any more," she answered, and this time when she went to pat my head, I didn't swear at her.

"We have to stop," I said.

My mother nodded. We were both miserable and ashamed.

I was placed on Ritalin. This was the word — "placed" — that the doctor used and that was readily accepted by my mother. Ritalin, the doctor said, was a medication for hyperactivity. It was experimental, though not in any way dangerous.

My mother, on hearing that her son was about to be placed on experimental medication, was ecstatic. According to the doctor, my condition was entirely of my own making and yet, the doctor assured me, beyond my control. It was certainly not caused by bad parenting.

Sitting in the doctor's office, I wondered if he'd have said the same thing after having spent a week with us. As it was, we'd only just met, but this did not seem to deter him. The cause was not of consequence. The remedy was three pills a day, every day for six months.

My mother, in what I thought was one of her few questions of substance, asked how the pills worked. The doctor answered by saying that Ritalin was a form of speed which, for those who were hyperactive, had a calming effect.

"We don't really know why it works," the doctor added. This, I gathered, was the experimental part of Ritalin. Since I had never heard my father admit ignorance on any subject to which he attached importance, I was surprised that the doctor would admit his own. My father would have had no time for such a man. My mother, unfortunately, was desperate and strangely susceptible to men with expertise, even those who admitted to their failings. With prescription in hand, we walked out of the doctor's office and straight into the pharmacy conveniently located on the first floor.

My mother wrote a note to Mr. Bunt, asking him to excuse me first thing each morning. I'd quietly rise from my desk, walk to the water fountain, and extract a pill from a piece of crumpled tinfoil. Within minutes I was enveloped in a world tinged the colour of bright urine. This was a side effect no one had bothered to mention. The main effect was harder to gauge. I never saw the doctor again and my mother, after her initial rapture, failed to mention my daily dosage, though she placed two pills in tinfoil each day without fail.

My excursion to the water fountain made me suspicious of every other body leaning over for a drink. I looked to see if they placed two pinched fingers into their open mouths, the telltale sign for Ritalin takers.

Strangely, my haze offered me greater clarity, and I soon noticed that others in Mr. Mitchell's class were enveloped in the same yellow fog. Weinstein for one. He no longer made the quick cuts from left to right with his eyes. Now when Mr. Mitchell said "come," his eyes rolled in a wide slow arc, sometimes plunging from top to bottom when the exertion became too much.

I also began to realize that Juan's bush-jumping was an act. He'd throw himself into a bush without provocation, waiting for me to berate him while I stood there on the street wondering what possible protection a stark winter bush could offer. His complexion, suitable for summer, now made him look unwashed and impoverished. Although I didn't have a clear idea where Chile was, watching him shiver in the bare branches, the snow entangled in his hair, I knew it was a long way from here. So did Juan. This knowledge had stunted him. He was unimpressed with Mr. Mitchell, uninterested in his hardships, and unwilling to discuss strategies to avoid his wrath.

To my surprise, Mr. Mitchell appeared equally content to ignore Juan. A part of me believed that Mr. Mitchell, a man of dark skin, would acknowledge a fellow sufferer, but after a few initial thrusts directed Juan's way, Mr. Mitchell left him alone.

Juan's displacement was enough; he didn't need Ritalin.

Despite my medication I still tortured Foxy Lady, rolling her down hallways, then chasing after her to offer solace and companionship. She retreated to my father's study and one day followed him out to his car, where she jumped into the back seat and allowed herself to be transported to the university undetected. A colleague of my father's, a woman, discovered Foxy Lady sitting on his office chair, panting in eager anticipation. She pleaded with my father to let her take Foxy Lady away and, in an act of magnanimity and foresight not usually displayed by my father, he called the house to ask for our consent. He understood, like my mother and I, that Foxy had made a great, even noble escape. It was something to admire; what else could we do but let her go.

Without Foxy Lady to torture, I began to torment my mother with new-found enthusiasm. "Fuck you, cunt!" became a familiar greeting, and she would often smile before her eyes clouded over in anger and shock. The Ritalin made my utterances sound sluggish and soft, and I began to think of my tongue as a worn elastic band, often imagining that I could taste the stale rubber in my mouth. I sensed that my father, who often masked his indifference with a look of bemusement, was truly at a loss when it came to my swearing. He gave me a lecture about the nature of Anglo-Saxon swear words, stating that the Germanic root of the language offered a sharp, direct path to the bowels of humanity.

This was all the protection he could provide for my mother, and it was clearly inadequate.

One day when returning from school, I found my mother sitting upright on the living-room couch, a cup of coffee held between her hands. She was listening intently to a man with sandy blond hair whom I'd seen before and associated with a large, disorganized office full of books. He greeted me by my first name.

"You remember Jack McClelland, don't you?" my mother asked.

There were two other people in the room and I recognized both of them — one was Sylvia Fraser, the other Anna Porter. I also noticed an oversized notepad on the

table with a few furious scribbles written across the page
that I took to be my mother's.

Like the scribbles on the notepad, there was something frantic and indecipherable about my mother's voice
which carried throughout the house. Even the solid door
of my bedroom was unable to withstand her insidious
excitement.

The meeting ended shortly after I returned, my
mother sweeping up the cups and small cakes which lay on
the table. As the weeks progressed, the meetings became
more frequent and the clutter on the living-room table
more cumbersome.

Without being told directly, I learned that my
father was about to be given a surprise sixty-fifth birthday
party. There were a few details that I picked up: it was to be
at Casa Loma, a large castle often used for parties. There
would be a lot of people; my father would love it.

Since this event was to be a surprise, my father was
not to be informed. Secrecy was uppermost in my
mother's mind and sharp warnings were issued to all par-
ticipants. Not being formally told about the party
excluded me from my mother's admonition. I could have
ruined everything by simply walking up to my father and
letting him know what was planned, but such a thought
was as far from my own mind as it was, evidently, from my
mother's.

That I knew something my father didn't made a
particular impression on me. We didn't keep secrets from
each other; we *were* the secret, each of us unfathomable to
the other.

What had begun as a damp shine in my mother's
eyes now became a bright, almost permanent glow. It was
the difference between a puddle of water reflecting light
from a lamp and the lamp itself; one you could stare at

easily, the other only with great difficulty. These, I knew, were eyes to be wary of. I'd last seen them while standing on the bare attic floor that was now my father's office, and I quickly ceased tormenting her. It wasn't because I was scared of being punished; I simply understood that in her present condition, my torments would have no effect.

But where I had seen a strange unyielding strength in her determination to move from one house to the other, I could now sense only an uncomfortable weakness. Then, her happiness had been at the expense of my father's. Now she was dependent upon it.

Jack McClelland was my father's publisher, a role I was only vaguely familiar with, but which I knew was identified with much of my father's happiness. He was quite unlike anyone in my own family and made me aware, by his gracefulness, that he felt sorry for my mother. I had become accustomed to my father's bursts of charm, but Jack exhibited less charm than manners, his way, I thought, of pretending not to notice the nervous tics which had recently exploded all over my face.

Anna Porter's face was dignified and composed. This was not a face one swore at. Sylvia Fraser's face was much more like my mother's, vulnerable and exposed. The three of them — Jack, Anna, and Sylvia — huddled around my mother, the unquiet centre of her manufactured storm, and helped prepare the secret birthday party for my father. Each of them looked at my mother in ways that revealed a dark knowledge of our family, of the life which held us captive in this house, the life which I was vaguely aware was poisoning me.

And which, until now, I had believed was a tightly held secret.

One day my father took a hoe to the back of the yard and vigorously began to break up the soil. He was going to plant a garden. "Make things grow," was the way he put it, and he explained to me that when he was a child his family had always tended a plot of land devoted to growing vegetables. Vegetables — in his mouth the word sounded crude and elemental.

"It's important to work with your hands," he said, standing shirtless beneath the summer sun. I couldn't help feeling that he somehow wished to punish the soil, to rip it apart.

"All the neighbours did it," my father went on. "Anyone with a plot of land." In those days, my father assured me, growing food was a necessity. He called this endeavour farming, and used the same word to describe his present activity. My idea of farming had been developed by school textbooks: large wheat fields groomed by giant red machines. Still, the elemental lessons seemed to apply — fortitude, patience, and foresight.

My father handed me a shovel.

"Each seed needs to be nourished like a word upon the page," my father said, scattering seeds haphazardly across the mounds of clotted earth. The truth was that his stubborn embrace of the earth seemed to lack all the qualities associated with farming. His was a sudden endeavour, without the correct tools, and with no appreciable knowledge of the earth's peculiarities. My father was tilling some of the most expensive real estate in Canada for a pound of pitted potatoes and a radish or two. We were doomed to failure.

"Give me the name of a general. Can you think of one?" my father asked suddenly.

"Napoleon. He was a great leader," I said.

"Nonsense," my father answered.

"But he was," I went on. "He conquered Europe!"

At this boldly stated fact my father could only grimace.

"They come and they go," he said, bending over to grab some weeds. Could I remember anyone else? Besides Napoleon? My father's doubt was a challenge.

"Attila the Hun!" I yelled excitedly. "Churchill! Caesar!" Then the greatest name of all came to me, the one I knew my father could not deny. "Hitler!" I shouted.

"Exactly," my father said in response, delighted by the wide selection of names I had offered him. "And do you know why you've heard of them?"

"Because they were important."

"Son, the warmongers, the paper-pushers, the crafty bureaucrats, are nothing but fodder for the minstrels."

"Then why have I heard of them? Why are they so famous? They must have done something!"

"Have you heard of Shakespeare?" my father asked.

"Yes."

"Then that's why you've heard of Julius Caesar." My father pointed his toes to a mound of earth. "Dig here," he commanded. "It's always good to learn a skill," but I stood staring at his deeply scarred right tit. It was my father's most important feature and after each exposure I felt as if something had been revealed to me. He'd had the scar since childhood, when a lighted candle had caught hold of his nightgown and ignited it. The flames had deformed the right side of his body and turned the skin into angry knots of flesh. Without his shirt, there was only one thing helping to cover the scar and that was his medallion — the Hand of Fatima.

I waited, along with hundreds of others, behind the massive front doors of Casa Loma. The rooms, populated with hollow suits of armour, were hushed in anticipation of my father's arrival. Under the stone frame that surrounded the door, between the throne chairs that sat on either side and beneath the immense paintings, I felt as if I were in a giant's lair, anxiously awaiting the sound of a key being slotted into its keyhole.

The castle, I had been told, was the manifestation of one man's love and ambition. Moved stone by stone from Scotland, it was reassembled and offered as a home to his new bride. The endeavour had bankrupted him, a circumstance from which he never recovered. Another story of house-mania, I thought, and a fitting place for my mother to throw a party.

"Shhh, they're here."

This was said by several people at the same time, the words echoing through the huge crowd. Finally there was complete silence.

"Just a moment, Irving," I heard my mother whispering as she tried to direct my father's footsteps towards the door. Her intimate tone was not intended for the large public gathering which surrounded me, and I felt strangly excluded.

"Surprise!" shouted the crowd.

The first light to flare was a television camera which caught both my parents in its bright gaze. Illuminated, my mother's dress sparkled, while my father confronted the crowd with a wide, angry smile.

"My God!" he exclaimed.

"Surprise!" the crowd shouted again.

"Happy birthday, Irving."

My mother's words were accompanied by a delirious smile. As the main lights went on, I was pushed forward by the crowd. She placed an arm around my shoulders and watched my father make his way to the centre of the room.

Jack McClelland climbed up on a podium, called for silence, and announced that the prime minister of Canada, Pierre Elliott Trudeau, had sent a telegram. The telegram was read and then a large cake was wheeled into the main room. Sylvia Fraser popped out of its centre and planted her red lips on my father's mouth.

As the waiters glided through the noisy crowd, each with a crown of drinks perched over his head, I followed behind them, occasionally feeling the white heat of the camera lights as they swept through the crowd.

My father was no longer standing among his guests but had retired to a high-backed chair, an over-sized pen in his hand, huddled over a piece of paper. He was like a bullfrog on a lily pad, serene and content but ready, at a moment's notice, to lash an unsuspecting victim with his tongue. Naturally, I kept my distance, and so, I noticed, did everyone else. The party swirled around him while my father, apparently oblivious to all, prepared his speech.

Another telegram arrived.

"This one is from Leonard Cohen," someone shouted. The crowd quickly quieted down, until there was a silence far deeper than the one for the prime minister.

"Irving," Jack McClelland read from the telegram, "you and I will never grow old."

"Never grow old?" I thought. I found the words meaningless. My father already *was* old. But the words were also beautiful and, like everyone else, I smiled.

My father was still in his chair composing, but he lifted his head and steadied the crowd with a wide smile before returning to his work.

Then it was time for the speeches. Moses Znaimer,

the person responsible for the white glare of the camera lights, now stood on a raised pedestal, the white collarless shirt beneath his black jacket giving him a priestly look.

"Let me tell you about the first time I met Irving," he said. "I was a student at Herzaliya School. On the first day of school my new teacher strode into the classroom, walked straight to the blackboard, picked up a piece of chalk, and wrote in large figures the number 99.9999. He then turned around and asked the class what that number represented. When we didn't answer, he shouted, 'Ninety-nine point nine nine nine nine percent of humanity are sheep! Followers! Only a small percent are artists, and they're the only ones that matter.' Then he threw down the chalk, stared hard at the class, and growled, 'You choose what you want to be.'"

Moses turned to Irving.

"Irving," he said, "you've ruined my life. Because of you, my success feels worthless."

Since I'd always imagined that the only life my father had tried to ruin was my mother's, the fact that he'd taken time out to ruin the lives of others was a revelation. Moses' cordial accusation against my father signified a certain intimacy, and I found myself oddly envious of him. My father couldn't have ruined my life: it would have taken too much time.

I walked over to the bar and ordered a Coke. The man behind the counter was preparing for a renewed onslaught, placing bottles of wine in plastic tubs of ice and asking others to remove the empty beer cartons that lay at his feet. As I waited, the first words of my father's speech echoed through the great hall.

"When Aviva insisted I wear clean underwear this evening, I should have realized that something was brewing."

By the time the laughter subsided, I was already in another part of the castle, the voice of my father muffled by the thick walls and heavy carpets of Casa Loma.

I was attracted by a strong white light at the other end of a large rectangular room. As I walked towards it I passed a wall composed entirely of shelved books encased in glass cabinets that reached from floor to ceiling. I looked for a sliding ladder but couldn't find one. The books above, it appeared, were permanently removed from the hands of curious visitors. On closer inspection, I realized they were made of a continuous line of plastic and that the titles were painted on.

Leaving the plastic books behind, I came to a glass-walled room with a gleaming marble floor and green plants which banished the sombre gloom of the castle. Soon others from the party joined me, glasses of wine in their hands, and the room became filled with words, laughter, and music.

My mother joined me on the white marble floor. We began to dance beneath the glass ceiling, while my father far away on the other side of the castle held court.

I failed Grade Seven. It was my mother who notified me of this unfortunate setback, and it was with her that I walked silently up the street to my school, now emptied of students. I found out that Juan had also failed. He walked out of the principal's office with head hung low, while I sat waiting my turn. I had invited him to my father's birthday party, but had spent the night avoiding him. Now I again tried to avoid him as he walked out, a look of defeat on his face.

On entering the principal's office, I took a chair

which was beside, but slightly behind, my mother's. Mr. Bee, the school counsellor, sat behind the desk. Throughout the year, Mr. Bee had attempted to pollinate morons like myself with the seeds of his wisdom but, judging from the number of students outside, without much success. It was, I felt, the Ritalin, which made all things infertile.

I barely listened to my mother and Mr. Bee. Their tone was prearranged, their words leftovers from a previous conversation. I was involved in a ritual and, knowing its outcome, I ceased to be interested. I would not fail. My mother had already seen to that. Unlike Juan, I was protected by privilege.

We were leaving for Greece the next day. My bags were already packed.

Chapter 3

TREADING WATER

Nada threw a party on the second night of our arrival
in London. It was a tribute of sorts to my mother's
yearly migration, but it was also a party for all those who
would follow my mother, a signal that summer was here
and that London was the centre of the world. Nada's
apartment was a kind of marker, a starting point upon
which I measured all subsequent travel. Still, I never knew
where I'd end up. And neither, it often appeared to me,
did my mother.

For the first time, I was no longer able to slip
beneath the Moroccan covers and allow the crowds to swirl
around me. My feet, my legs, my entire body had become
too large. Instead I was forced to be amongst the crowd,
watching people suck smoke down their lungs.

The usual suspects were at the party, plus a number
of new faces which, to my mind, were all interchangeable
from years past. A Canadian who worked in television, an
American who worked in film, a Hungarian piano player,

a Japanese stamp collector. They were all brought together, or kept together, by Nada, who was constantly branching out her hands, touching one then the other, so that her body was the trunk which rooted all these people to her floor.

Nada's guests sat on her bed, on my divan, on the floor, scratching their chins, stroking arms, shaking hands. It was overwhelming and impossible to retreat from, a world filled with its own excitement.

"Why am I so tired?" a man exclaimed. "I can't keep my eyes open." But he could.

"Duncan," a woman shouted from the next room, "you've been on a plane for seven hours."

"But all I did was sit and eat."

"That's all you ever do."

Before he could answer, a woman, on all fours, began to rub against Duncan's legs.

"*Meow.*"

"Katy! What the fuck are you doing?"

Katy purred and then gently shook her head, so that the fine strands of her white-blond hair brushed against his pants.

My mother caused me the greatest concern. She spent her time in the bedroom, sitting on the edge of Nada's bed, talking to a man with an alarmingly prominent forehead. He wore a kerchief tied with an elaborate knot around his neck and a jean jacket embroidered with coloured starbursts. I distrusted him immediately. Far worse were my mother's eyes; they were brighter than the brightest star embroidered on the man's jacket.

Something was happening between the two of them, what Nada commonly referred to as a "connection," and which perhaps explained the bulging vein on the man's forehead. It became so engorged with blood that a small tributary developed to help divert the overflow. My mother did absolutely nothing to shield me from this sight, a point which should have alleviated my concern but instead ignited it. I was sure my mother had something to hide; she just didn't, as yet, know it.

Every so often, the two separated, but every time they walked into different rooms they seemed incomplete, either too idle or too frantic.

Eventually, the party began to wind down, as people picked up their jackets and bags and disappeared out the front door. Those who remained retired to the kitchen, including the man and my mother, who turned off the lights in the bedroom and tucked me in before leaving. As in years past, I lay in the darkness and listened to the sounds of laughter from across the hall which every so often became brighter, as someone opened the bedroom door to pick up a forgotten item.

"I've resigned myself to the fact that I'll never leave Irving. I'm with him to the end."

This proclamation came from the kitchen. Late morning light was streaming through the window, and as I opened my eyes I noticed that the bedroom had been thoroughly cleared of last night's party. My mother and Nada had already been up for some time.

"It's not a matter of good or bad," my mother continued, answering a question that, as far as I could tell, hadn't been asked. "It's not as if my life with him is like a book I can put down. My life with Irving *is* a book," she said with growing enthusiasm. "We're both characters in a book, and I could no more leave him than jump off the page."

75

Over the next few days, while my mother and Nada passed their time in the kitchen, I spent a great deal of mine sitting on the divan looking out the bedroom window which ran almost from floor to ceiling and had metal bars running across its frame. Several lawn chairs sat out in the damp grass, the seat cloth of each chair sagging low to the ground. I also kept my eye on a metal bucket, encased in another metal bucket, which I was sure hadn't been moved an inch since the previous year.

The view of the garden was partially blocked by an outdoor staircase leading to a second-floor apartment. I'd never seen it used but, on the fourth day, I saw a bearded man lying on one of the lawn chairs, his chest and arms exposed to the clouds, and knew that he had descended from above. Nada, when asked, said he was a heroin addict who was presently being administered methadone from a medical clinic. I had only a vague idea of what she was talking about, but felt nevertheless that this helped explain why he looked so out of place amid the deep green of the garden. Only his teeth, grey as the sky above, connected him to his surroundings.

Although the outdoor staircase clearly gave the heroin addict certain rights to the backyard, I felt that he was an intruder and wanted Nada to claim her proprietorial rights. After all, we didn't have heroin addicts sunning themselves in our Forest Hill backyard. Instead, she carried a bowl of pea soup out to the garden and placed it on the ground, where it remained untouched.

"He's harmless," Nada said, walking back into the bedroom. I hadn't meant to be caught looking out the window, either by the heroin addict or by Nada, but the odd look of blank concentration which covered the man's face had been transferred to my own. Nada's comment irritated me — I was no longer thinking about the man in sight, but about the woman who wasn't: my mother.

Nada had told me she'd left early that morning, while I was still asleep, but I had an unsettling suspicion that she hadn't arrived back the night before.

"Where is she?"

"She's out seeing a friend. She'll be back soon."

I was already taller than Nada and had to bend my head down towards her. "I think something's happening."

"Nothing is happening. Nothing at all."

"Please tell me," I said.

"I'd tell you if there was," she said sternly, as if to say that she was not a woman who would be caught in a lie and certainly not one of such great importance.

"Nada," I said, following her out into the hallway, "I think . . ."

But she slipped through the garden door and out of my reach.

Straight ahead of me lay a damp cubicle where an English toilet — it was more a well than a toilet — sat to the back of one wall. I felt that at any moment I might fall through the hole. Worse, something else might crawl back out. Toilets, it became clear to me, were just the gaping mouths of sewer pipes. Back home, our bathroom possessed a toilet of white enamel complemented with a matching sink sculptured in the form of a seashell. It was harder in that house, my home, to make such unpleasant connections.

My mother took me to Hamley's, a toy store off Oxford Street. With her talent for admiration, she described the toy store as the world's biggest, a claim she'd made every year and one I'd taken seriously until now. I was bored and, making my way through the clutter of stuffed animals, hanging airplanes, and brightly coloured boxes, I couldn't help feeling that my mother's behaviour towards me was careless, as if I were one of those paperbacks she'd dog-ear and then leave behind on the beach. My mother failed to notice that I'd outgrown the toy store, much as I'd outgrown Nada's divan. She stood to one side of the entrance and looked possessed. As I passed her on my way out she gave me a wan smile and followed behind, as if I were the one who could lead her through the high streets of London.

We ended up at Camden Market. I entered the crowded dirt lanes that inexplicably held great appeal for my mother and passed stalls crowded with clothes, trinkets, and boxes. Boxes for spices, boxes for makeup, boxes for jewellery, boxes made of wood, boxes made of metal, of plastic, even paper.

My mother, sufficiently recovered from her odd stupor, led me to a stall that had army fatigues and dented candle holders. Two women worked behind the covered table: the one with dark hair was called Joan, the one with blond hair, Jenny. According to my mother, they'd been at Nada's party, but I didn't remember them.

"I remember you, David," Joan said, winking at my mother. I wasn't sure if this statement referred to just the party or stretched further back to some past summer, but I had a vague recollection of this place, of the clothes and stalls and the woman frying hamburgers at the market's entrance.

"You're such a flirt, you can't remember all the women you meet," added Joan. Then she offered me a bottle of crushed seeds from the table, saying it would be good for my pimples.

"Crushed guava is also good for the skin," added Jenny.

While they discussed my skin condition and listened to my mother's worried interjections about blackheads, a girl my own age stood nearby. She was clearly lost in her own thoughts but any minute, I feared, she would return and find me surrounded by concerned women.

"Dania, come and say hello to Aviva and her son David." At Jenny's command the girl I'd been staring at swung her head in our direction, but her attention was diverted by a customer pointing at one of the shirts. I watched as she helped the man fit his arms through the sleeves and then, in an act both intimate and professional, button the top portion of his shirt. It occurred to me that I hadn't worked a day in my life.

Dania, her customer satisfied, turned to scrutinize my skin. "It's all that greasy food Americans eat," she said with great authority. Her comments were directed to my mother, who readily agreed.

While Dania went away to fetch another customer, I clutched my bottle of crushed seeds, hoping that a great plague would descend upon her skin. Then I would pour the abrasive paste over Dania's face and scrub hard until there was nothing left.

That evening, as my mother sat soaking in the bathtub, she informed me through the half-opened door, and then only as if it were an afterthought, that she'd be leaving me with "Auntie Nada" for the evening. There was a measure of calculation in the way she told me, as the words spilled and mingled with the sound of running water. It was the water, and not the door, that acted as a barrier between us, a barrier which she needed; unlike the night before, my mother was now aware that she had something to hide.

I listened to the sounds of her preparation: a hand foraging through a bag of cosmetics, a razor pulled across a leg, the snap of a bra. When it came time to leave, my mother kissed me on the cheek and, almost at the same time, looked knowingly at Nada who was standing behind me. Then she walked down the hallway, towards the front door, gone before she had even left.

Panayottis, the village garbageman, who, so my mother insisted, had been well over a hundred, was dead. He had passed away in the spring and would no longer be leading his horse through the cobblestoned streets of Molyvos. My mother took his death as a sign; people were dying and with each death a small piece of the village went with them; the wooden garbage buckets strapped across the horse's back would themselves become trash and the songs which accompanied the disposal of our household garbage would no longer be heard.

Our arrival each summer — even the threat of our arrival — seemed to precipitate a death in the village. There had been the Cretan, a man with a great white moustache who carried tourist luggage up the steep slopes of Molyvos and died in the middle of winter, when the tourists had no need of him. And there had also been Stella, who had poured kerosene over her body, lit a match, and set herself on fire.

My father had written a poem about her, about how she'd been the most beautiful woman in the village, had been hated for it, and had left with an Athenian poet who eventually deserted her. She returned years later to the village, penniless and abandoned. I'd always known her as an old woman, her legs grotesquely swollen by ulcers, who sat each day on her front stoop and watched the vine-covered street grow light and then dark with the passing of the sun.

Mankind, my father declared, was afflicted with a black heart. "They despised her beauty, for what they couldn't have and what she wouldn't give." Despite this rather bleak assessment, I noticed that my father's cordial relations with the villagers — Stella's tormentors — remained unchanged. As for my mother, she had always treated Stella's death with more interest than concern.

That a villager or two dropped dead each year was a kind of tradition. So why, this time, did my mother find the garbageman's death so unsettling?

"Things are changing," my mother complained.

We were sitting on plastic-covered couches which made rude noises each time we moved our bodies. These couches, along with the linoleum floor, played a significant part in my mother's present unease. With my mother, houses were the clue, and the newly renovated house we now found ourselves in this summer was not like those we'd rented in the past. With its level floors and painted shutters, we were in a kind of Forest Hill of the village.

My mother, out of choice or necessity, had always chosen houses further up in the village, houses which in most cases were falling apart. Often, I had been able to lie in my upstairs bedroom and stare down through the rotten floorboards to the rooms below. There had been a house with a Turkish toilet, and another with a belching kitchen sink that released a foul odour. But these smells didn't bother my mother; I suspected she enjoyed them.

My mother had no need of Forest Hill except when in Forest Hill. In the dead of winter, often with a Ritalin hangover, I'd curl around a portable radio and listen to Greek programs; the distinctive echo employed by the announcers to heighten the sense of urgency, the bouzouki music. I listened to it all, though I couldn't understand a word. And my mother sometimes joined me, sitting on my bed and staring out to my unprotected deck.

"Soon. We'll be there soon."

And here we were.

Against the plastic-covered couch, I noticed first the darkness of her skin, then the darkness of my own. I placed my arm on the back of the couch and lifted it. Up, down, up, down. All I needed to do was flap harder and I'd rise from the couch, glide out the window, and take off for the open sea.

My mother and I had been among the first foreigners to arrive and it was her job, as it was every year, to find a house and set it up with dishes, food, sheets, and towels. I'd occasionally accompany her to the village stores, where I used my time to procure as much as I could for myself — miniature sailboats, oversized chocolate bars, boxes of cornflakes — until I lost patience and made my way down to the beach.

My mother never lost her patience and the house was soon filled with what she called the "necessities." My father, fresh from some previous encounter, arrived around this time, though the specific date and time was never conveyed to me. I would simply run in and find him, as I did this year, sitting on the couch, reading. Like the house, he arrived ready-made, the final and most important of my mother's necessities.

My mother claimed that there were no other houses available this year and hinted that this too pointed towards a change in the village, but I felt that she brought her strange ailments with her; the house we now rented was simply a symptom rather than a cause of her present uneasiness.

"Avivoo!" My father's voice came booming out from the other side of the front door and was accompanied by the sound of a chair being pushed to one side. "Avivoo, where are you?" With this, the door swung wide open and in came my father from the beach, his pants stained from the wet swimming trunks underneath. Seeing the stain, my mother smiled.

"Guess who I bumped into on the way back to the house. Leon Whiteson, you remember him, don't you? He was struggling up the hill with his suitcase." My father turned his head towards the front door. "Leon," he shouted, "come in, come in."

And in walked the man with the alarming forehead, suitcase in hand, a wide, wild grin on his face.

"I told him he can stay for a few days, while he looks for a place in the village."

My mother's smile was completely wiped off her face. Perhaps out of nerves, or perhaps because I felt my mother should somehow suffer, the smile on mine had just begun.

Our move was prompt and efficient. What my mother had claimed was impossible was done seemingly within hours of Leon's arrival. On the morning of our move, I ate breakfast in one house, and by early afternoon, I ate lunch in the other.

Our new house fronted onto a small side street that smelled of sun-baked stone and flour. There was a large courtyard, roofed with a mesh of vines, which my mother energetically swept with a twig broom.

"Isn't this wonderful?" These were the words uttered by my mother every time I walked through the courtyard gate. She seemed to be perpetually startled, my entrance always a surprise, and when she spoke to me I had the feeling she was expecting someone else.

There was a large pomegranate tree out on the street, visible from one of the chairs in the courtyard. It was where my father sat when he was in the house, but now it was mine.

"It's ... wonderful!" I shouted, in imitation of my father. "Couldn't be better!" I raised my arm and gave a theatrical bow to the courtyard.

This gesture, along with others I'd performed over the last few days, not only disturbed my mother, it disturbed me as well.

"Have you been having a little sweep?" I asked, repeating a phrase I'd heard my father use the previous day.

There was a smile on her face, but it was unsure of itself and I knew it could easily be moved to either laughter or rage; even both at the same time, if the conditions were right.

"Have you seen your father?"

"He's playing chess down on the beach." Actually, this was a lie. I hadn't seen my father at all, either down at the beach or in the tavernas, but I knew that these words would inflict pain. I watched as my mother took a step backwards, then a step forward in an attempt to regain her original position.

Leon played chess and, from what I'd come to understand, had played chess with my father in the past. Since I had no memory of him, I developed one, moving him and others around like the chess pieces on the board until Leon and my father were facing each other across the table at Ramona restaurant, a chessboard between them, a plate of olives and feta to one side.

My father often sat at the beachside restaurant playing chess, so it wasn't hard to place the two of them together. He'd proclaimed Leon to be a "fine player," and Leon had returned the compliment a little too vigorously, by saying my father was a "genius," a point my father didn't dispute.

My mother had put the broom away and was already walking towards the front gate.

"Where are you going?" I asked.

"I didn't realize how late it was getting. I'm going to see some friends who've just arrived."

I lifted myself out of the chair and followed her out onto the street. Ordinarily, I wouldn't have bothered, but I was too immersed in the pleasure of tormenting her to let her go.

"Who are we going to see?" I asked.

"Duncan and Elizabeth. They're further down the village on Cemetery Street."

This was the name my mother and I had given to one of several roads leading towards the walled cemetery that lay half a mile out of town. Peggy was buried there. She had once let me paint beside her, on a small canvas that took me all summer to fill. Her spine was twisted, which caused her head to hang to one side and made me wonder how she drew the large paintings that were stacked against the walls. Greek garbagemen weren't the only ones to die in the village; foreigners died too, and my mother spent a morning each summer sitting quietly beside Peggy's grave.

I had never liked the houses on these roads. They were too large, with empty fields beside them, and there was often a dull wind blowing, just enough to stir up the dust and dirt of the street, but not enough to blow it away.

Duncan and Elizabeth lived in one of these houses. It sat alone, squatting in one of the empty fields. A large car was parked outside, a Volvo station wagon, which had been driven straight into the field. A picture of the Statue of Liberty was imprinted on the licence plate.

I followed my mother up an outdoor staircase leading to the second floor of the house.

"Aviva! Where have you been hiding?"

It was Duncan, the man I'd seen at Nada's party in London. He had a ball of dope in one hand and a lighter in the other.

"You just missed our dark prince," he said.

"But Duncan," my mother answered, "you're my dark prince."

Her reply provoked laughter from two women standing to one side of the room. One woman had sandy blond hair, looked somewhat malnourished, and was sucking on a cigarette. I took her to be Elizabeth. The other woman was Nada.

"Why don't you make yourself useful," Elizabeth shouted to Duncan. Then she turned to Nada and my mother and added, "I've been trapped in a car with this man all the way across Europe."

"You're an *asshole*. You could have rolled out of the car any time."

"You never stopped the car long enough." Elizabeth sounded tougher than Duncan, more on edge.

"I never stopped the car? Elizabeth, there isn't a field in Europe you didn't piss in."

"On. Piss on."

"In. On ... there's going to be massive crop failure this year. Fallow fields across Europe. All the rains of Noah couldn't wash away the piss you left behind."

Elizabeth gave a surprisingly stylish snort through her nose and left the room.

Duncan was still holding the ball of dope and the lighter, which he now lit.

"You smoke dope?" he asked.

My first impression was that he had shifty eyes, darting constantly from one object to the next, but now, when I actually looked at them, I found two still pools of dark liquid.

Duncan didn't wait for an answer. His ball had been sufficiently warmed and he began to crumble the hashish over a piece of rolling paper already layered with tobacco. I fixed my eyes on the crumbling flakes.

Duncan lit the joint and gently placed one end of it in his mouth. "Where's the great man?" he said, releasing the smoke from his lungs.

"Irving's on the beach," my mother replied.

"And our dark prince?" he asked.

"If you mean Leon, he's not here."

"I heard Leon stayed with you before finding a place with Nada," Duncan replied slyly.

My mother wagged her finger at him.

"That's why we never stopped the car!" Elizabeth shouted, entering the room with several drinks in her hand. "He wouldn't let us. He was frantic from the moment we met him in London, pleading with us to give him a lift to Greece."

"It's true," Duncan interrupted. "'We have to get going, we have to get going.' That's all the man said. All the way through France, through Italy. He drove us crazy, didn't he, baby."

"You drive me crazy," Elizabeth replied.

"He left us for a bus heading straight to Athens. We weren't going fast enough for him. Can you imagine? He deserted an air-conditioned Volvo for a bus. Well, he's here now. Nowhere else to go. The dark prince has arrived."

I left, while Duncan began to roll another joint. A donkey was standing beside the car, tethered to a door handle. Like the other donkeys in the village, he looked exhausted, and stood passively beneath the hot sun, his surprisingly delicate eyelashes shielding his eyes from the glare.

Katy and Paul were the next to arrive in Molyvos. They parked their VW van on the side of the road leading into town, pitched their tent, and began to socialize. Their two children, several years younger than I, slept in the van, on a king-sized mattress elevated off the floor to allow for storage underneath. Clothes, propane canisters, cooking pots, even spare headlights had all been thrown into the van's belly and tossed together on the long drive from London. It was a dark, messy, and exciting space to peer into.

The evening of their arrival everyone assembled for dinner at Manoly's, a taverna in the agora. I caught sight of Dania. My mother had failed to inform me of Dania's imminent arrival, one more omission I was forced to confront. Dania's presence made me angry. I'd been given no warning.

When our food arrived at the table I promptly took the plate of tzatziki and moussaka which I'd ordered, circled the plates with my arms, and began to eat.

There were many plates of moussaka, as well as an assortment of other food placed haphazardly across the table, but these were for use by all.

"David doesn't like to share his food," Nada said.

"You're selfish," Dania added, sticking her bread into a communal tzatziki bowl and smiling.

"But I don't want anything of yours, I just want what's mine!" I shouted.

My mother turned to look at me. "It wouldn't hurt to share," she said. There was a look of concern on her face but there was also something else: a smile? She had, as I feared she would, betrayed me.

The truth was, I despised their cult of sharing. I wished no foreign fork to spear my food and had no desire to plunge my own into the food of others. The thought nauseated me.

In defiance, I pulled out a package of Cadbury chocolates and stuffed a large piece in my mouth.

"Aren't you going to share your chocolates with us?"

When I refused, Dania, playing to the crowd, asked, "Not even with me?"

"These are my chocolates," I said sternly. "If I was smart enough to bring them with me from London, then I should be the one to eat them. If you had any, I wouldn't ask you for some."

"You're a spoiled American," Dania said.

"An angry American!" shouted Duncan, triumphantly.

It was then that I noticed my father, sitting at the far end of the table. I'd forgotten he was even there, hunched over his food and listening to Leon, who looked drunk, mad, or both. It occurred to me that Leon wouldn't have dared place a fork anywhere near my father's food. My father was always the final arbiter as to when he should be the centre of attention, and right now it seemed that he wished to disappear.

I left the table for the street and Dania joined me. We both looked back at the adults in the courtyard, at Jenny, her mother, at mine, and then at my father.

"Would you like a chocolate?" I asked.

"Are you sure you can spare one?"

I placed a piece of chocolate in her hand and watched as she placed it in her mouth, along with several strands of her blond hair, which she chewed along with the chocolate. By the time she had brushed back the hair with her hand, I could think of no one else.

It was Dania's first time in the village and we began to organize picnics, arriving early in the morning at Mr. Big's, a grocery store named by foreigners for the man who stood behind his calculator, his whirling machine constantly clicking out the bill of his latest sale and further depressing the Sad Brothers, two brothers who owned the store next door: although they sold the same produce as Mr. Big, they never received a customer.

We bought peaches and grapes and, out of what I took to be an extraordinary act of compassion, even went next door to buy bread and honey from the two sad men. We walked to the main road past the olive groves, stopping first at the Delphini hotel for a drink of lemonade by the pool and then continuing to the petrified forest where we squeezed through the barbed wire and picked up coloured pieces of petrified rock even though the signs forbade it.

We were soon high up on the coast road, the blue sea beneath us, sticking our thumbs out at the occasional car which passed by. A taxi driver picked us up, unconcerned that we had no money to offer him, and began to sing, taking his hands off the wheel to clap in time to the music on the radio as we swept along the winding road.

"In Greece we love!" he shouted, patting me on the shoulder and grinning. "We love!"

I knew that if he'd caught his own daughter on the road he'd have thrashed her but we were foreigners, *xeni*, and the rules didn't apply to us.

In the town of Petra, I took Dania up the 413 steps leading to the church and told her, proud I knew the story, that it was a shrine to the Virgin Mary, who'd rescued a group of sailors from a great storm by depositing the boat on the massive rock we now stood upon. Then we stepped through the door where the smell of candle wax and incense mingled with the heated peaches in my backpack.

Several tavernas lined the main street of town overlooking the water, and we sat at one of the wooden tables and sipped Cokes before making our way down a small road that ran along the water's edge. Leaving our belongings on a secluded stretch of beach, we ran into the water and faced each other at a depth where our feet barely touched the bottom. I placed my hand on her belly, rubbed it gently, and then slowly moved it downward. The pleasure of having my hand tucked beneath her legs was overwhelmed by hers resting between mine, but soon the two sensations equalized and I stood floating in the ocean, my outstretched hand exploring the murky life which lived below.

"Could you help Katy? She's under the table again."

I didn't recognize the man who made the request of me. It was becoming impossible to keep track of all these new arrivals. They arrived and, within hours, became regular fixtures on the beach and at the taverna.

"Tell me where she is." I kept eating my way through a package of *loukoumades*, fried doughnut batter soaked in honey and cinnamon.

"We last saw her at Alepou's, but when I tried to get her out she scratched me. She won't tolerate adults." The man showed me his arm. Three red tracks, like those left by cat claws, marked his skin.

Katy had begun to walk around the VW van with her tits exposed and, more recently, had gone down to the town beach in the same condition. I'd never seen Katy's exposed breasts myself, but now a more troubling condition had clearly emerged. Katy dived under tables and begged like the village cats for scraps of food, rubbing her body against the legs of diners. When I found her, she'd obviously been under the table for some time; the diners were doing their best to ignore her but they looked irritated.

I took a piece of fish off a plate, bent down, and offered her the delicious morsel in my outstretched hand.

"Here, Katy," I said, speaking to her as I would to a cat. "Pssss, pssss, pssss. Katy." The words excited her and she began to rub fiercely against the legs of the diners. "Mmmmmm," I cooed, looking at the food I held in the tips of my fingers. "It's good. Good food."

Katy gave me a wide smile but it wasn't really one of recognition. Though I found her actions worrisome, there was no denying her talent.

"C'mon, Katy," I said, backing away from the table as she began her crawl towards me. "C'mon."

I stopped when I reached the street and waited for her to poke her head out the taverna door. Then I scratched her head and listened to her loud, contented, and surprisingly authentic purr.

"You're a good cat," I said.

She laughed.

"Why don't we go back?" I suggested. "It's time."

With each step, Katy began to transform herself back from beast to human, relaxing one muscle and tensing another so that by the time we'd travelled the short distance from one taverna to the next, the metamorphosis was complete.

Largely ignored by everyone, Katy took her seat. One person who did notice her was Nada's boyfriend, Brian. He had shockingly white hair which rose off the top of his head like a steam cloud — Duncan called it the greatest Afro he'd ever seen on a white man — and was, my mother assured me, a professional mime artist, who'd studied in a famous mime school in Paris.

Brian rose from his chair and silently bowed, as Katy and I entered. He'd taken a vow of silence which he swore he'd maintain for the entire summer.

His very last words — "There are too many writers!" — were a kind of proclamation against noise and chatter. This was met with thunderous applause, especially from the writers, my father included.

"Bravo!" my father shouted. "We should listen to him more often." My father's joke caused everyone to laugh, except Brian. Unable to respond, he was already beginning to disappear.

I ordered lobster. It was my thirteenth birthday, my Bar Mitzvah, as my mother repeatedly stated. I was allowed to order anything I wanted, and for once I knew I wouldn't have to share my food. Unfortunately, I hadn't been consulted about the guests and, while Brian was included,

Dania had been overlooked. I sat at the head of the table
and felt strangely inconsequential, even embarrassed. I'd
been to several Bar Mitzvahs back in Forest Hill and had
always been astonished at the massive preparations — the
Bar Mitzvah boy suddenly breaking into liturgical song;
the assembled guests who'd travelled from places like
Pittsburgh and Atlanta; the great hall reserved and
adorned, all for one small boy. In contrast, I sat at a
wooden table, its legs propped up with matchboxes to
prevent it from wobbling, with a bunch of strangers who
knew either less or more about what was happening than I
did. And anyway, there'd already been one Bar Mitzvah in
our family and it had gone to my father on his sixty-fifth
birthday.

"How do you like your lobster?"

It was Leon, and I found his question vaguely
threatening.

"I like it very much," I answered.

"Here's to the crustacean family," he said, raising
his glass in the air, "more edible than a golden calf."

"And far more expensive," added Duncan.

Everyone laughed, except my mother. She was
sitting beside Leon, and I watched as he lowered his wine-
glass and moved it beneath the table. When he returned
his glass to the table it was empty; he was quietly pouring
wine onto my mother's lap. Everyone was busy talking and
eating, even my mother, but the damage must have been
substantial. Her dress was white and Leon's wine a deep
blood red.

Leon, I noticed, looked rather pleased with
himself. He slowly poured himself another glass of wine,
then lifted it in the air and offered a silent toast to himself.

"My God! Look at Duncan!" somebody whispered.

Duncan was leaning against one of the restaurant

doors, with a glazed expression on his face. There were several red lines running down his right forearm which I took to be scratch marks. Then I saw that the red lines on his forearm weren't scratch marks at all, but tiny rivulets of blood.

"How'd he get the stuff?"

"From Turkey?"

"Maybe he bought it here."

"Impossible."

Duncan hadn't moved and neither had anyone at the table.

My lobster was soon strewn across three plates. I discovered that a great deal of it was inedible, including its protruding eyes, two withered black currants dangling from their stems, staring directly at me.

I swivelled the lobster head towards my father, my mirror image, sitting at the other end of the table and the only other person with a lobster in front of him. Once again, his presence came as a surprise. That was the strange thing about my father; I was always suddenly noticing him.

As I sat there staring, I tried to recall an actual conversation with him and failed, although I knew there were numerous occasions when they must have occurred. I could place my father: sitting in the courtyard, preparing coffee in the kitchen, lying on the beach. And I could hear his voice deliver a phrase, a statement, a pronouncement or two, but nothing more substantial. I found very little of what he said usable, and what was usable failed somehow to live up to its initial promise. Just like the lobster.

Nada was sitting beside him, picking at his scraps of lobster meat. He wasn't a man who allowed people to eat off his plate and, when he failed to respond, it was then that I knew: my mother and Leon were having an affair. It had been obvious without being clear. My father knew as well; I'd used his eyes to see what was happening.

I got up to leave, wondering where I could find Dania, and as I turned, I saw my father walking towards the toilet, looking older than those around him, with a kind of frayed dignity that I found ridiculous and frightening. Still, I thought, at least he's able to move about. My mother, unable to move for fear of revealing the wide, red stain between her legs, remained stuck to her chair and eyed my father with a strange mixture of sorrow and envy.

"Son, your mother and I are having our difficulties."

My father pulled up a chair for me in the kitchen while he remained standing. A pot of coffee was on the stove, the white flames licking the metallic sides, but there was no food, either on the table or on the kitchen counter. In years past I had been expected to make my way to the bakery and bring back fresh loaves of bread, but this year my mother had taken over full responsibility for our needs, delivering breads, fruits, and yogourt to our greedy hands each morning. I often waited for her in the court-yard as she swept through the front gates, panting, her hair like untended vegetation, wearing the same clothes as the night before.

"I've got some wonderful food, some yogourt, grapes, and lovely fresh bread." It was the same every morning and didn't need to be repeated. Then, exhausted, she walked to the kitchen and prepared breakfast. I never offered to help.

But today my mother had failed to put in an appearance. We, my father and I, were alone and without food. The kitchen looked remarkably empty without all that food. There was something even sterile about it.

"I'm sure you've noticed problems between us." My father had now taken a seat and was staring directly at me, something he rarely did. It was unnerving. Problems? Did I notice problems between them? Did he mean now, this summer? Was the question limited?

"I noticed," I answered.

And I had. Hadn't I asked my mother, each morning, if she'd slept well, and hadn't her discomfort pleased me? And didn't I avoid my father, fearing his embarrassment? And hadn't his embarrassment pleased me? I'd been in a kind of collusion with my parents without ever really knowing that I knew.

My father continued. "Sometimes two people, even if they love each other, fail each other. This is what has happened between your mother and me. She's found another man. A younger man," my father added. I hadn't noticed the age discrepancy between Leon and my father, but then I remembered him shuffling off to the toilet on the night of my birthday party. He did look old, but it seemed self-imposed.

"Are you getting a divorce?" I asked.

"Well," my father sighed, "I think, for a time, we will be separated and then we'll see. But it will be difficult for all of us. I just wanted you to know."

"Thank you," I said. Tragedy, even his own, brought out the best in my father.

After this there wasn't much else to say. I couldn't help feeling that our presence somehow damaged the room, which seemed to become more desolate with each passing moment. We were essentially inadequate for each other.

I wanted to move out into the courtyard but I couldn't find the means of lifting my father off his chair.

Suggesting we sit outside sounded a bit too presumptuous. Should I have taken his hand, placed mine on his shoulder? Should he have done the same to me? My father blew hot air over the lip of his coffee cup while I sat wondering how I could extricate myself from this room and from my father. A towel, hanging from one of the kitchen chairs, provided me with the necessary prop. Swinging it over my shoulder I told him that I was on my way to the beach for my morning swim. My father waved me off.

"Good!" he proclaimed. "Get some exercise."

When I returned later that day the kitchen, which previously had been so quiet and sombre, was now the centre of a great eruption which could be heard far down the street.

"It was only fair to David," I heard my father say, as I walked into the courtyard. "He had a right to know."

"You did it for him? For *him*?" my mother shouted. "Most of the time you can't even remember his name."

"There's no point pretending any more. David knows."

"No use pretending? You've been pretending all your life. Pretending to be a husband. Pretending to be a father. Pretending to be in my bedroom when you were really in someone else's. Actually," my mother continued, suddenly contradicting herself, "I don't think you've ever bothered to pretend, I'm just giving you the benefit of the doubt."

"Enough, Aviva! I can't talk to you like this." These words were delivered to my mother in the weary tone my father always adopted when feeling unsteady. He induced hysteria, admired it, and was therefore terrified by it.

"But you can decide to talk to your son, without

first discussing it with me, can't you. 'No use pretending'! Pretending!" This word set her off again. It enraged her.

As I listened, I couldn't help feeling that my father had made the right, and hence surprising, decision this morning when he had sat me down and informed me the end was near. My mother couldn't help thinking there was a hidden motive for my father's actions, and perhaps there was, but there was also an immense confusion clouding his thoughts: he had needed me this morning, a clear indication that things weren't going right in his head.

The cats, all three that we'd adopted for the summer, gave my position away. They prowled back and forth from the kitchen to the courtyard, rubbing my ankles and somehow bringing my scent to my parents. Where there had been great noise, there was now silence. I coughed.

"David? Is that you?" It was my mother, her voice filled with a false cheerfulness.

My first instinct was to flee, but I held my ground and answered back.

She came out, her hands patting down her hair, a habit she'd picked up from her morning dashes, and exclaimed that I'd arrived just at the right time for lunch. My father failed to put in an appearance, retreating instead to his room, where he remained for the rest of the day.

That night, as I lay in bed, I heard someone tapping on his windowpane.

"*Meow.*"

The window was pushed open and Katy slipped into my father's room.

My mother placed more of her time at my disposal. Her failure to arrive with our bread and yogourt had led us to the precipice, but now she was determined to pull us back from the edge. Breakfast was delivered. So was lunch. Even her hair, such a clear indicator of her mood and state of mind, was now tamed. And her voice had lost none of its enthusiasm, only its hysteria. It was possible to believe, at certain times of the day, that nothing had happened. My mother, not my father, was now the master of pretense.

It was during dinner, the candles flickering over the courtyard table, that my mother's work was destroyed. A puff of air was all it took to send the shadows racing across my parents' faces, and then it was possible to see what the sun had hidden. The fork in my father's hand moved mechanically from plate to mouth. Only his lips, agitated with the excitement of the food, showed any life. The rest of his face was immobile. My mother preferred to stare at her food but every so often she'd raise her head, usually right after my father smacked his lips, and look at him as if she didn't know who he was.

At first I assumed her presence was to keep me out of trouble — as her son I was not to be violated with the truth — but I soon suspected that it was the other way around; she needed my presence to keep her out of trouble.

As part of my mother's new regime, I accompanied her to a swimming cove that lay twenty minutes from the town cemetery, along a goat and donkey path. After paying her respects to Peggy, whose bent, crippled body lay just beneath a small tombstone, my mother and I walked along the thistly path and commented, as we always did, on how close Turkey appeared, its rugged coastline so near it seemed we could swim across. Squinting, I wondered if, on the other side, two other people were walking along a similar path, staring at us, wondering who we were and where we were heading.

The pebbled cove was studded with several boulders jutting out at the shoreline, as if chaining sea to land, and as I peered over the cliff's edge to find the downward path, I noticed several women lying on the bare stone. Halfway down, I could make out dark patches of pubic hair, and gravity-flattened breasts, still white despite their exposure to the sun. They reminded me of pancakes, and the dark patches of pubic hair skillets to cook them on.

Cynthia was among the unclothed women, lying naked on top of a boulder. She was only a year older than me, but far more developed, with a sadness, a kind of lethargy, that marked her as someone to be avoided. Her parents were divorced or dead, I couldn't quite make out which, but they weren't here in Molyvos.

Cynthia had arrived in the VW van with Katy and Paul, who'd taken her in for the summer. She slept on the elevated mattress in the van and sometimes, in the morning, Dania and I would peer through the windows and watch her sleep, her body curled up in a sheet, her dark hair tangled around her face. She didn't have the right to her privacy, as I did, or Dania, and no one was going to offer it to her.

I didn't say hello to her on the beach. As I was the only male at the cove — and the only person with a bathing suit — the division between us was so huge I barely acknowledged her presence. Besides, my attention was focused elsewhere, on a woman who lacked pubic hair. Noticing my stare, she casually informed me that she was infested with crabs and needed to rid them of their natural habitat. "I took their little Eden away from them," she explained. Though she'd shaved her pubic hair, there was still a faint outline where it had once been. I wasn't sure if this was caused by a natural discoloration of her skin or by the emerging stubble of new hair but, fearing a similar affliction, I moved away.

I didn't think it possible that such a thin layer of pubic hair could cover up such a catastrophe. She told me that anyone, man, woman, or child, could contract the small vermin, but I was certain there'd been a reason why they'd chosen her. My own few strands of hair appeared far too insubstantial to support such teeming life.

Having examined her vagina the best I could, given the quick, furtive looks I allowed myself, I decided to enter the water, swim, and then re-emerge directly in front of her, or perhaps just to one side, in order to gain a more thorough view.

I swam towards one end of the cove where there was a cave. A sea lion was supposed to live here, but no one was sure. I heard the water lap up against the rock and listened to my own breathing, which echoed in the chamber. Then I heard my mother.

"I can't leave him."

Her voice came from the other side of the point. I realized I'd been so concerned with the bald vagina that I hadn't even noticed if my mother had made it down to the cove with me.

"Listen, I'm not going to play games with you and you're not going to play games with me." This time it was a man's voice. Leon's.

There must have been another small beach tucked away in the cliff and it was close by, because I could hear every word. How had my mother reached it? Had she swum there? That struck me as too extreme. There must have been a separate path down, which would explain how Leon had arrived without detection.

"I'm not 'playing games,' as you put it. I just don't know what you want."

"You don't know what I want? I want you! This time, you're not going back to that man. That gorilla."

"Don't be adolescent. He's a great man, whatever his faults. A great poet."

"The man's an emotional thief."

"He needs to be," my mother said. There was a note of cruelty in her voice, the tone of an ally being slighted.

"Jesus, this is the kind of poison he's fed you all these years. It's killing you."

"He hasn't 'fed' me any poison, Leon."

"Then you're willingly killing yourself?"

"I'm not 'willingly' anything."

"You're defending a man who takes other people's pain and turns it into clumsy poems!"

"Well, which is it?" my mother shot back. "That he's an emotional thief or that he writes bad poetry?"

"Why are we always talking about that man!"

"It seems that *you're* always talking about that man. It's not about Irving anyway. It's about David. This is very difficult for him and he needs some stability."

I hadn't expected to hear my name. It sounded strangely foreign — my mother talking about someone else who happened to be me.

"You're doing this for David? If you don't do something soon he'll end up in a lunatic asylum."

Incredibly, my mother laughed.

"Don't use your own son to hide behind, it isn't fair to him."

This stranger, who had poured wine over my mother's lap, who had some unknown right to yell at her, and who threatened to destroy my father, was now defending me. To my surprise, I felt grateful.

My mother was momentarily speechless.

"All right," she finally said, "It isn't for David, it's for Irving. I can't leave him now. Maybe ten years ago, but not now. I can't do that to him."

"You see? The biggest child gets the biggest carrot. That's why your son will be in a straitjacket. He'll always be the one to be sacrificed."

I was getting tired from treading water, just as I used to get tired from squatting on the upstairs landing in Forest Hill. It didn't matter that I was floating in a cave, the coast of Turkey behind me and a sea lion below, it was always the same. I was forever eavesdropping on my fate.

"I'm leaving," my mother said.

"I fucked Vicki."

"How could you?" my mother wailed. "She has crabs!"

"I fucked her afterwards."

A pair of feet pushed off from the stones and then I heard my mother's voice, more distant this time, shouting to him, "It's a betrayal."

"Is it?" Leon yelled back. "You haven't spoken to me for a week. And if you won't leave Irving, why should I wait? I'm not some pawn in the sick games you two play!"

I spent a few more minutes paddling in the cave before emerging back into the sunlight and swimming slowly to the cove. Vicki was still in the same spot, leaning on her elbows. My mother was beside her, talking. The anger, the screaming, had collapsed in the few short minutes it must have taken her to walk back to the cove. I came closer to shore, looked at my mother, looked at Vicki's bald vagina, and then looked upwards towards the cliff face. Leon was standing on its edge, glaring fiercely down at me.

That night my father burst into my bedroom and declared that he'd written a poem of "unquestioned genius." My mother had disappeared again and it was just the two of us in the house. He began to read the poem, taking great care to point out what he called the "shades of meaning." I hadn't had time to lift myself out of bed so, as he read from the white page he'd just yanked out of the typewriter, I swung my legs over the side of my cot and pulled the sheets over my hips.

I thought he'd been asleep, or out of the house, but then realized I'd heard the tapping of his typewriter only moments before he'd entered my room.

He sat opposite me on a spare bed that I often fantasized belonged to Dania, and read me his poem. At first I was confused by his presence but his voice, steady and appreciative of his own words, began to have an effect on me. When he was finished, he asked me questions about the poem. They were good questions and I did my best not to answer them. I was an inadequate audience for my father; it was only desperation which led him to me.

There were a few more questions my father wished to put to me before leaving my room, but these were ones I wasn't expected to answer. He seemed to be talking to himself, comparing the poem he now held in his hand with others he'd written in the past, even with those he hadn't yet written.

He talked about "themes" and "ideas" like Mr. Mitchell, but I couldn't help feeling these were of secondary importance. They certainly were to me. The only theme that came to my mind was my father, sitting shirtless on the bed, his great scar searing down the right side of his body. Compared with this hairy, maimed animal beside me, the flimsy sheet of paper which he held in his hand was barely interesting.

"I can't blame your mother for leaving me," he said in what I took at first to be a change of subject but then realized was simply its continuation. "I'm a poet, and who can live with poets?"

I wasn't asked to reply.

"It's impossible. If your mother hadn't left me, I would have pushed her out. Cut her loose!" he shouted, suddenly excited by his generosity. "She's a young vibrant woman with her whole life ahead of her. Poets!" he spat out in disgust. "We must forever remain unencumbered. That was my mistake."

I was surprised that my father aligned himself with a group he held in such contempt.

Just then a fly landed on a spiral piece of flypaper which dangled from the ceiling.

"You see, my boy, the more they struggle, the more embedded they become."

My father turned from the fly to me.

"Do you remember when I read you bedtime stories?"

I nodded. "Shockit," I said, referring to the rabbit my father invented, and whom I still occasionally dreamed about.

"Shockit!" My father laughed, delighted by the name. "You used to like those stories, didn't you?"

I nodded again.

"Goodnight, son."

"Goodnight, Dad."

I heard my father's feet shuffle down the hallway and then the sound of a door opening and closing. Even though he was only a few feet away, in another room in the same house, I couldn't hear him. After the staggering noise he'd made in my room, there was now only silence.

My father had left behind his poem, which dangled over the edge of my mattress. A puff of wind must have pushed it over the edge, but the paper failed to yield to gravity. Crisp and inflexible, it thrust itself in my direction, demanding that I pick it up. I didn't bother.

There was in my father a theme of sorts, but not the kind Mr. Mitchell ever taught in his class.

Dania and I had begun to get into ferocious fights that never seemed to be fully resolved; it was as if we'd become infected by the adults surrounding us. One evening I met her and Cynthia at the village movie theatre, wearing, as I always did when arguing with Dania, my best clothes. In my breast pocket were a pocket knife and a plastic skull which conveniently emitted a beam of light powerful enough to temporarily blind someone.

The Guns of Navarone was playing for the second time that summer. When the Greeks in the movie lifted up their fishing nets and bagged several Germans in their speeding motorcycles, we stood up in our plastic chairs and threw pistachio nuts. I called Dania a "Nazi."

After the movie, Cynthia followed Dania's indignant march down the street but soon left us. I suspected she grew bored with our theatrical hatred for each other, and I pretended that it bored me as well.

"Let's stop playing games," I shouted at Dania, suddenly furious at our stupidity.

"You're the one who threw food over me. And you called me a Nazi. You're a child," she added. "A baby."

To regain my lost stature, I took Dania to Stella's house and pointed to the spot where Stella had last been seen alive.

"Stella used to be the most beautiful woman in the village and everybody hated her for it."

Dania stood beside me but remained silent.

"My father wrote a great poem about her," I said, wanting to impress her. "She was too beautiful and that wasn't what people wanted."

"What happened to her?" Dania asked.

"She burned herself to death. Right here," I said, pointing with my foot at the cobblestones beneath me. "Let's go in."

I took Dania's hand and led her down a narrow alleyway running alongside the house. There was a small backyard with a stone fence, crumbling back into the dry soil, and a window, boarded with rotten planks, which led into Stella's one-room house.

After crawling through and allowing time for my eyes to adjust to the darkness, I noticed a chair standing in the middle of the room, the same chair, I imagined, that Stella had used to sit on her front stoop, the same chair she'd burned herself on.

"Come in, it's OK," I whispered to Dania.

I saw her head poke through the hole and helped her, grasping first her head, then her shoulders, and finally her hands, until she was all the way through. We seated ourselves on a backless couch, careful to avoid the straw poking through the upholstery, and sat staring at the lone chair. Despite the obvious signs of neglect, I felt as if nothing much had changed since Stella's death; the room mirrored her own decay.

In the gloom of Stella's house, with her empty chair as witness, I reached out my hand for Dania's breast, more for comfort than anything else.

The mime went missing. He'd shot out of the village on a motorcycle and had failed to return. No one thought much of his absence until the second day, when word came back that a foreigner fitting Brian's description was in hospital, apparently suffering from severe head injuries.

It was reported that the man could open his eyes, even smile, but was unable to talk. The doctors feared the worst.

The hospital was in Mytiline, the island's capital, and Duncan offered to drive his Volvo into town. I joined Nada and my mother in the car, a slightly dangerous proposition because, as I'd discovered in Morocco, I could never really be sure where we were going or if we'd return.

I sat in the back seat with my mother, and as we sped along the twisting roads of Lesbos, it occurred to me that Leon must have sat in the same place on his way from London, must have seen the same cypress trees, the same villages, as I now did.

Duncan had a cigarette burning between his fingers — he seemed to be steering the car with it — and refused to stop singing "Hit the road, Jack," until we all joined him.

"We're off to see the mute cripple!" he shouted.

He appeared to be delighted by Brian's misfortunes, calling him heroic.

"And in what better place," he added, "than in the land of heroes."

We passed through a pine forest, high in the hills of Lesbos. It was my favourite place on the island, the most mysterious, and I secretly wished I could stop the car and get out. It was far from anything Dania and I had explored, but I hoped to return and lead her through the woods.

"Hey man, no daydreaming." Duncan was peering at me through his rear-view mirror. "That's what causes accidents." Then he turned to Nada. "Your man's a day-dreamer and look what happened to him."

Despite his interest in Brian, Duncan stayed close to the hospital wall when we reached his bed. Nada and my mother were the ones to reach out and touch his bandages. Several doctors and nurses were also around the bed, having followed us from the reception desk. They were intrigued by his symptoms but had already begun to suspect their source. The nurses smiled indulgently when their patient twirled his foot. He had found a new audience.

Despite the clear pleasure he gained from all the attention, he had a look of stubbornness on his face. His body was deeply bruised, he was in pain, but he refused to utter a sound.

"They need to know what's wrong with you," Nada said to him. "You have to tell them what hurts." Brian just smiled. "Why don't you write it down?" Nada reached into her purse and brought out a piece of paper and a pen. "Here," she said, "take it."

Brian extended his arm, but an imaginary wall interfered. Then he shrugged as if to say he'd done his best, but a wall was a wall and there was nothing he could do about it.

Bored, Duncan leaned over and asked me about Dania.

"So, how's your girlfriend?"

This appeared to be a serious question but I couldn't be sure, so I shrugged my shoulders. It was more of a flinch than a shrug and I felt my lack of style must have been a disappointment to Duncan, bored as he was by the activities in front of him.

"She's a hot little number," he said and then quickly smiled, a kind of wink of the mouth, before sighing. "Ah, Greece, you can fall in love with a fucking donkey here."

Dania offered me her toothbrush. The blue stem sprouted wide, soft bristles which I placed in my mouth, tentatively at first, but then, finding the sensation oddly pleasurable, I pushed them flat against my teeth and scrubbed vigorously. My attraction to Dania's toothbrush kept me enthralled for several minutes before I finally spat out the white foam in my mouth.

Dania was beside me, in her pyjamas, clearly interested not in her toothbrush but in the person using it. She kept staring at me, startled that I was in her bathroom, at night, while she stood beside me, waiting for her chance to lean over the sink.

As we switched places, I noticed that her pyjama pants were held together by a cord which knotted in front. Mine had always been held up with elastic bands and the difference struck me as profound. The shape of her pants was more delicate, more formed, even exotic. She wasn't wearing underwear.

It was our last night together and I was spending it in Dania's bed. Her mother found this act disturbing and kept asking us, in a voice which became increasingly shrill, to be careful. I wasn't entirely clear what she meant, though each time she shouted at us I looked at Dania and smirked.

Jenny not only alluded to some great disaster which might befall us, she indicated a first-hand knowledge of what that disaster might be. As we moved down the hallway and into Dania's bedroom, Jenny's voice followed us, though she herself stayed in another room. She seemed strangely powerless, unable to prevent what she most feared. She could have told me to leave, or at the very least demand that I sleep in another room, but her requests became increasingly irrelevant; as we closed the door behind us she yelled, "Dania, I want you to do the dishes," but we slipped into bed and ignored her.

The door closed; we were inviolable. Jenny would no more walk into this room than Dania would walk into hers. It was part of an understanding they had, although what that understanding was based on, how it worked, and who was at fault for its flaws, I couldn't say.

There were stars in Dania's bedroom. I'd seen them before, during the day; a stick-on package of half-moons, spinning Saturns, and pointed stars that spread themselves along the side of the wall. I'd thought it childish of Dania when I'd first laid eyes on them but now, in the darkness, an entire universe unfolded in front of me.

"They glow in the dark," she said, while we tried to adjust our bodies to the strange sensation of being so near each other. The stars helped, opening her room up to a limitless world. We stared at them for a long time.

Then I slipped my hand underneath her pyjama top.

My previous encounters with Dania's breasts had been hurried, rude inspections with no chance for proper exploration. But now, by the very act of being in bed with her, I was given not only permission, but possession. They were mine, though they were hers, and this odd fact imposed a certain discipline on the encounter. What exactly were these mounds on her chest? Her breasts were certainly larger than mine, but not nearly enough to explain the preposterous difference I felt lay between us. I could have circled my fingers around the tips of her nipples forever. I was reminded of a small net I used when trying to catch fish. I'd stand a few feet offshore and drag it through the water for hours. But why? I couldn't eat the fish, they were too small. And anyway I could see them in the water, so what compelled me to pull them out?

The cord which tied Dania's pants around her waist ended in a large front bow. These were very much her pants. I was entitled to only half her body: the wooden stick of the fishnet.

I started touching her feet. I'd never really looked at those either, and touching them gave me the same unforeseen pleasure as placing her toothbrush in my mouth. My mother was forever trying to get me to rub her feet, squealing with delight whenever I applied the slightest pressure. I clamped Dania's toes with the palms of my hands and squeezed, working her feet as if they were my own.

"Come here."

The sound of her voice startled me; I'd somehow forgotten she was there.

"I want to kiss you," she said.

As I slid my body back up, I left my hand behind, lodging it between her legs.

"Don't, it's wet."

Wet? I rested my fingers over where I imagined her wet spot to be and pushed down. Something was warm, but wet? I pushed down some more, felt a slight patch of moisture, wondered if it was the sweat of my own hand, and then pulled away. The tone of her voice had unnerved me; it had a dark, mature intimacy that made me think of Cynthia, sunning herself naked on the rock, and of her damp, black hair. There were some things that were best left unexplored.

I saw Dania off at the bus, shaded from the morning sun by several olive trees which branched over its roof. A few bags, some boxes, and, oddly, a toilet bowl were piled on top. She climbed up the steps, waved from the window, and then turned away just before I lost sight of her. I looked for some impression, some clue that she'd once stared through the window, but couldn't find one and felt betrayed. She hadn't stared hard enough. There was no sign of her, no residual fog from her breath. Nothing.

I waited until the bus turned the corner and the last puff of black exhaust smoke had blown away before making my way back. The quiet streets, dappled by the early sun, made me feel as if I'd just returned from a long voyage and, in my absence, the village had entered a period of slow decline. With sword in hand and a great red Roman cape across my shoulder I stopped, the returning warrior, to buy a bar of chocolate.

My mother was sitting in the courtyard, reading.

"Did you see Dania?" Her female sympathy disgusted me.

"Where's Dad?" I asked.

"What do you mean?"

"Is he here?"

"Is he where," my mother answered warily.

"What the fuck's wrong with you?"

"Please don't swear at me." Apart from the real fatigue I heard in her voice, this came out more as a request than a demand.

"Where's Dad?" I asked again.

My mother cocked her head to one side, looked at me, and said, "He's not here," then continued staring at me as if to observe the results.

"When's he coming back?"

"He's not coming back." The look on her face told me that whatever confusion she'd just suffered from had passed; she was withholding information for the sheer pleasure of it. I started to walk away, knowing this would flush her out.

"Your father left two days ago," she said. "You didn't know?"

"No."

"Your father left the island two days ago and you hadn't noticed?" This was not an accusation and I wasn't forced to reply. "You didn't notice?" she said again. My mother obviously thought that a little piece of magic had just been performed. My father had the ability to disappear without being noticed. Who the magician was in all this was hard to see, but I began to wonder if anyone had bothered to tell me that he was leaving — my father, for instance. Had I forgotten? And if so, how had I failed to notice his lack of presence in the house?

"No, I didn't notice." I saw Dania's face staring at me from the bus window. Why did she turn away before I was out of sight?

"He's in Hydra," my mother said, making me feel she was answering a question I should have already asked. "With Leonard."

My mother had abandoned my father, and my father, in consequence, had abandoned me. I knew little of Leonard except this: my father called him "my boy," and he understood my father's poems. I didn't understand my father's poems. Worse, I didn't want to. He'd come into my room, recited his poem, and left, unsatisfied. Now he was on another island, had left me behind with *the women*.

"I can't believe you didn't notice," my mother said

once more, but I was fed up with her incredulity.

"That seems to be more your problem than mine," I answered sharply.

My mother cast her eyes down on the patio floor, then her head slumped forward.

"No," she said quietly, "it's both our problems."

I couldn't see her face, but I knew she was crying when I saw the part in her hair — a long, white, wide gash.

Chapter 4

NEW BAGGAGE

My mother usually heralded her arrival at the front
door of our house on Delavan Avenue by stamping
the snow off her feet and crying out a two-note greeting;
this time I heard only the heavy thud of the door as it
closed behind her.

I'd been vaguely aware of my mother's departure
but, like her arrival, it had been unannounced. One
thud of the door and she was gone, another thud and she
was back.

I rolled off the bed and walked to the landing. My
mother was nowhere to be seen. Instead, I found someone
else at the door, his body encased in a gigantic coat — a suit
of armour made of fur and leather. It flared at his waist
then plunged to the floor. His head was encased in a hat
with four fur flaps and in each hand he held a large suitcase. It was Leon.

"David?"

The timing of my mother's call was not by chance.

We'd learned to detect each other's lurks and stalks through the house. Crises were what drew us together; they were the only thing we noticed.

I ignored her call and kept staring at Leon, whose suitcases were anchored to the floor; he simply refused to release his hands from the handles. He was too preoccupied with the sudden heat of the house, with the house itself, to notice me.

Leon struck an imposing and determined figure, standing in the alcove wrapped in his immense coat, snow piled around his feet. He looked like a Russian officer and I couldn't be sure if he was about to attack or retreat. Either way, his path would herald a great swath of destruction.

"This is Leon. You remember him, don't you?" my mother said brightly, as she entered the hallway. I stared down at both of them. "From Molyvos," she added.

I backed away and returned to my parents' bedroom.

The answer to the question "Where's Dad?" had not, even after six months, been adequately answered. He'd arrived back at the house shortly after us, bellowing his welcome, and returned to his study on the third floor where he pounded furiously away on the keys of his typewriter. The autumn winds blew the summer air away, and Greece became a thin, distant sound from my portable radio.

My dosage of Ritalin had doubled. I'd calmly fixate on small household ornaments and stroke carpet plush for hours. My mother had dipped into my Ritalin as well, which disturbed me because she didn't have a prescription. She claimed that it helped her to "concentrate" but on what, she had trouble explaining. I was the one failing school, I'd remind her.

I'd been given Mr. Mitchell again. I couldn't be sure if this was done to punish me, forgive me, or reward me for my efforts, however futile, of the year before. Mr. Mitchell might have regarded my presence in a similar light but I was neither his worst student nor his best. I merely forgot my regulation-sized ruler from time to time and failed to answer his questions correctly. Hardly something that would keep him up at night.

But he'd reduced me. I was no longer lying beside Dania, no longer standing beneath an olive grove plucking the hard fruit from its branches. And, strangely, I missed Katy. She'd given me the power to transform her from animal to human. And I'd been the only one allowed to pet her.

Instead I was forced to listen, once again, to Mr. Mitchell's tirade about the five-mile walk through the jungles of Jamaica to his school. His talk no longer impressed me. What was his walk compared with mine? It was what lay on both sides of the road that interested me, but Mr. Mitchell was intent on telling me only where it led to. That was his story. Perseverance, strength, the dignity of hard work. It was "five damn miles" to his school, Mr. Mitchell said, again and again, and all those miles had led him here, to me. It was a sad conclusion to his journey.

My father would never have settled for anything so inconsequential. Like Mr. Mitchell, he strode purposefully along the road, but he believed it led to great heights. On the way up, he recorded what lay on both sides of the road without ever getting off it. Katy, Brian the mime, hairless Vicki, they were all what my father called "characters." "Fuck-ups" was another word he sometimes used. He was attracted, he said, to their wounds and limps — their "manias." My father was never fearful of them. He was, he said, fully inoculated.

And where was he? That was the question I put to my mother after I lay in bed and noticed the silence from above. The rattle from my father's typewriter had long since stopped and I wondered when it would resume.

"He's gone," my mother said, but she added nothing more, fearful of our last encounter.

"When did he leave?" I followed my mother into her bedroom, where she sat on a chair, delicately pulling out her earrings and placing them in a small cluttered dish.

"Three months ago."

She was looking at my reflection in the mirror.

"You didn't notice, did you?"

I shook my head. My father had disappeared again, had walked down the road and out of sight without my even noticing. This was a trick he played over and over again. *He* was the magician, and I was nothing more than his assistant.

There were several other dishes on my mother's dresser. They too were cluttered with odd bits of jewellery. Coiled necklaces, brooches, earrings, rings, all piled and tangled together. They reminded me of small, abandoned nests. If my mother was using Ritalin, she certainly wasn't placing her new-found concentration here.

I wondered, as I lay there watching television in my parents' bedroom, where Leon was going to sleep. There had been a disturbing silence since my retreat from the landing. I heard a few plates scrape across the dining-room table, an occasional footstep, but very little else.

My last memory of Leon was of him lying on the beach, in a skimpy black bathing suit, slathered in olive oil, which he applied from a bottle that sweated its grease on the surrounding pebbles. He was practically as black as his swimsuit, his skin glistening in the sun.

He wasn't as dark any more, but he still looked exotic. He couldn't really be downstairs, in our living room, I thought, talking to my mother. He belonged to Greece, to Nada's damp London basement, not here in Forest Hill. It was impossible.

I was lying on my back, my head bent over the side of the bed, watching television upside down, when Leon walked through the door. I knew it was a compromising position, but waited a few seconds before rolling over on the bed and facing him the right way up. He leaned against the door frame and crossed his arms, a wide savage grin on his face. It was meant to be noticed. I grinned back. Then he took a breath and nodded, without failing to take his eyes off me.

We were sharing a secret, but even though I was grinning, it was more his secret than mine. He walked slowly into the room and placed himself behind the television, which stood on a metal frame that could be pushed around on four small wheels. He waited while I resumed my normal watching position, chin resting on my palms, elbows sunk deep into the mattress.

We continued to stare at each other, until I momentarily lost interest and let my eyes slip down to the television. It was then that he informed me of his secret.

"*No more television!*"

Leon's thunderous words were accompanied by an explosion as the television crashed to the ground.

I stared at him in amazement, too stunned to move. He still hadn't taken his eyes off me.

"What's going on?" my mother yelled.

As she bounded up the stairs, I pushed myself to the back of the bed, until I was squatting on several pillows. My mother rushed into the room, saw the shattered television on the floor, then looked at Leon, who was standing behind the empty metal stand.

"What's going on?" my mother yelled again.

"He broke the television! He broke it!"

It was my mother's turn to be stunned. She surveyed the wreckage at her feet, repeating to herself, "What's going on? What's going on?" It was a good question, another secret that only Leon could reveal.

"There's a new law in this house!" Leon bellowed.

"A new law?" my mother shouted. "A new law! How dare you come into this room and frighten David."

"He's been frightened for a lot longer than tonight. And I can't say I blame him."

"Get out!"

But Leon held his ground behind the television stand, standing there as if on a high balcony.

"This," he answered gallantly, his arm raised, finger pointing to the ceiling, "is *our* bedroom. It's time for David to get off his mother's bed."

"And it's not time for you to get on it. This is our house — David's house — and he'll spend his time anywhere he likes."

"What's he doing here anyway?" I whined.

Leon faltered. For the first time he looked down at the damage he'd caused, and I could tell he was at a loss to explain himself fully. Doubt crept into his face. He'd meant to come into the house and take control, but perhaps he was no better than the rest of us. Obviously, by the look on his face, it was a horrific thought. We'll win, I thought. We'll defeat him. It wouldn't be long before he too would be doped out on my Ritalin.

I walked over to my mother and let her take me to my room. She remained behind while I went to the wash-room to pee and brush my teeth. When I returned, she was lying on my bed, exhausted, staring at the wall.

"I don't like him," I said to her.

I heard a grunt from the next room; Leon was trying to remount the television set.

"That will never happen again. You're the most important thing to me in the whole world."

Her anger returned as she lifted herself off the bed.

"You can watch TV anywhere you want," she proclaimed and then, perhaps inspired by her declaration, added, "including our bedroom."

But who belonged to "our"? Was it my mother and me? Was it my mother and father? Or was it my mother and Leon?

He was in that bedroom now, cleaning up the bits and pieces which had flown off the television set, my mother straining to hear his efforts. With regret, I realized that I'd already lost control of her anger. Her interest was with the man standing next door, and as she left to resume her attack on him, I no longer felt it was made in my defence.

Their argument, I noted depressingly, quickly became nothing more than a fierce discussion. He wasn't going anywhere, I thought, and despite what my mother might say, I knew I wasn't going to watch television in their room ever again.

"Yoo-hoo, supper's ready."

I was down in the basement, my refuge, when my mother called out for me. The forced delicacy of her tone could only mean trouble. I ignored her.

"Yoo-hoo, food."

She was now halfway down the basement stairs, slightly bent over, though her head was easily clear of the ceiling.

"Turn off the television, and come upstairs. We're eating." These were astonishing words, delivered to me as if by rote. I turned and glared at her.

"C'mon," she said, suddenly annoyed, "it's time

for supper." She retreated back upstairs hoping, I imagined, that her words held sufficient power to coax me out
of the depths.

Turn the television off? What the fuck was she talking
about? Suppertime was when I turned it on.

I couldn't remember the last time I'd been
expected to sit at the table; that I was expected to do so
now struck me as not only unjust but verging on the
demonic. This was Leon's imperious work — his idea — and
my mother, far from protecting me, was a willing accomplice. And who, I wondered, did my mother think she
was fooling, coming down here and pretending that my
presence at the table was not only expected but perfectly
ordinary? It was incredible; she'd brought this lunatic
into our house in order to show him how reasonable we
were!

I observed three ordered place settings when I
emerged from the basement. My mother was at one of
them, her rigid body — hands on table, back straight — at
odds with her face, which looked as if it had been vacated
by whatever dream she was presently lost in. At least one
thing was clear: my mother wasn't fooling herself.

Leon was standing at the kitchen counter, his back
to the table. It dawned on me that he was cooking. There
was a large pot beside him, one I'd never seen before, with
a glass lid on top. Steam was escaping from the sides. He
wore oven mitts.

"Help me with the plates, David."

Without hesitating, I walked over to the counter
and did what Leon asked.

"Take this to your mother." He handed me a plate
of food.

As if in a trance, I walked towards my mother and
placed Leon's food in front of her.

"Thank you," she said.

It was all so peculiar, I felt exhilarated. I wanted to serve my mother again.

Leon had concocted a stew of some sort, made with chicken and vegetables. The taste was different from anything made before in the house, and each mouthful conditioned me to his peculiar tastes; a piratical invasion I could not avoid.

"So how is school? Tell me what courses you're taking."

I was stunned. So was my mother; she giggled.

Leon made it clear that he expected an answer, something specific, even documented. I couldn't even imagine what to say and sat stupefied.

My father had occasionally asked about school, but he always remained impervious to the answer, at best grunting at my response, at worst launching into a tirade about the evils of modern education and the need to acquire a skill, any skill, that would keep "the wolves at bay." But never had he asked about courses.

"School is fine."

"What homework do you have tonight?"

Homework?

I looked at my mother for comfort and guidance. What was the man getting at? His words, so casual, produced a kind of rage within me.

"I don't have any," I said.

"He goes to the Learning Clinic," my mother suddenly blurted. "Or he used to go to the Learning Clinic, but he wouldn't go any more even though we tried.

"It cost a lot of money," she added, turning to me. "You said you wanted to go, and you were getting better. Didn't you say that you liked the teachers?" She turned back to Leon. "They're very good, they think David is very bright, we sent him there after the school recommended he needed to do extra work. They're the best in the city.

"Why don't you go back? C'mon," she continued cheerfully, as if enticing me to a game of cards, "I could call tomorrow. They really liked you there, your teacher said you could do whatever you wanted, you just needed some guidance."

"I went there for a week," I snapped back. "A year ago." This momentarily halted her attack, as her mind tried to count time with the same plodding accuracy her fingers sometimes counted numbers. She kept coming up short.

"It was stupid," I added.

"Stupid?" My mother cried indignantly. "I don't think it was the Learning Clinic that was stupid."

"Fuck off!" I snarled.

Leon's hand smashed down on the table. He lifted himself up off the chair and stared at me.

"Don't you ever swear at Aviva like that again!"

Considering his own recent antics — and those not so recent — I found his indignation strangely delicate, chivalrous almost, and my mother, who looked for a moment as if she were about to intercede forcefully on my behalf, remained frozen, confused as I was by his firm defence of her.

Leon began to shake his head. "Jesus, Aviva, leave the boy alone. I asked him a question. Let him answer it."

"I was only trying to tell him — " but she was interrupted by Leon, who raised his hand to stop her traffic of words.

"Enough, woman! Your son and I are talking man to man. No mommies."

"That's hardly fair," my mother squeaked.

"Enough!"

He commanded me again not to swear at my mother, and in return he would protect me from her.

"If she's bothering you, come and tell me. Leave each other alone."

My mother and I both nodded dutifully. As Leon sat down, still shaking from the encounter, my mother and I reached out for each other's feet, not to kick in anger but to suppress our laughter. Still, Leon had made himself indispensable. He was our referee and we needed him. I scooped up the last of Leon's curious food and asked to be excused.

If I'd barely been able to detect my father's absence, his presence, coming so soon after Leon's arrival, was hard to miss.

Returning home from school one day, I found him sitting on the couch, reading the newspaper, the steam from his coffeepot rising above the wall of newsprint he'd placed before him. He looked extremely comfortable.

This was as I imagined him, and now that he was back I doubted that he'd ever left. I placed my school bag on the floor and walked towards the kitchen where Leon and my mother were both propped up against the kitchen counter. It was as if my father's presence demanded that he be given more room than he could account for, and had squeezed the two of them against the wall. Circumscribed by the narrow space my father afforded her, my mother nevertheless was full of activity, grabbing jars from the overhead cupboards and furiously mixing their contents in glass bowls.

I was offered a generous welcome by my mother, who asked if I was hungry and moved to the fridge in anticipation of my answer. Leon remained immobile, as if standing in a crowded subway car, trying not to touch his immediate neighbour.

A sandwich was placed in my hand and I walked to the dining-room table, which had open views of both the kitchen and the living room. My father was still sitting on the couch, but he'd placed his paper on the floor and was quietly talking to a woman who was sitting close beside him. Their hands were on each other's knees.

This plump, red-haired woman hadn't been on the couch when I'd first walked through the door. I assumed she'd been upstairs, pissing in our toilet, but I couldn't be altogether sure. Perhaps she possessed powers of appearance and disappearance similar to my father's, though I thought that unlikely; she seemed too firmly under his spell to weave one herself.

I expected there to be a formal gathering of some kind, between the couple in the kitchen and the couple in the living room, thinking that the food my mother was so busily preparing was meant for everybody, but as time passed I could see no movement in either direction.

My mother occasionally called out to them, to ensure their needs were satisfied, but other than that their conversations and activities remained separate and confidential. It felt as if I wore a diving mask and was half submerged, able to observe two distinct worlds at the same time. Apart from the occasional call from my mother, my mask was the only thing binding the two worlds together.

One day my father came alone, a pile of laundry tucked beneath his arms, a dirty undershirt dangling from his hands. "Avivoo," he bellowed, and my mother came running, taking from him the clothes which needed to be cleaned.

While his laundry tumbled through its cycles, my parents sat together on the couch, their knees angled towards each other.

"Harriet's a good woman," was my father's guarded assessment of the woman I'd last seen him with, and my mother agreed, provided, she said, that Harriet made him happy. According to my mother, this was all she cared about, which made me think of Harriet as a kind of sacrifice.

Her good intentions were met with a nod from my father: "Yes, yes," he said and then moved on to another subject only to repeat, moments later, this dull attribute of Harriet's. He had a way of making a compliment sound damaging.

I was in the kitchen pretending to make myself some food, carefully creating the requisite noises to avoid their suspicion. I opened the fridge, then closed it. I pulled out the cutlery drawer and quietly rattled some spoons. I slid a plate across the counter. Still, I wasn't sure all this activity was really necessary. Their interest lay in each other and no one else; it was just possible that I could have stood directly in front of them playing the trumpet without getting their attention.

"And Leon's a good man," I heard my father say. But this, apparently, didn't satisfy my mother.

"He's a writer, Irving."

"The man has talent."

I was certain these words brightened my mother's eyes considerably, much as they would if she'd received a compliment about her son.

"He works hard, Irving."

"Well . . ." My father shrugged his shoulders, as if to

say that yes, of course, Leon must work hard at his writing.

If Leon was doing any work, it was being done in my father's study, which he'd seized upon arrival. It was hard to tell what he was doing up there, but every so often I'd hear the rhythmic snap of his typewriter, which sounded more melodic — made less of a pronouncement — than my father's typing. It was, I assumed, the sound of work, but was it also the sound of talent? I'd stand at the bottom of the landing, wondering. And I was sure that my mother, in her own way, was doing the same.

Leon was up there now, avoiding my father and his dirty laundry, which tumbled and churned on the second floor, directly beneath his feet. Staying clear of my father by occupying his study appeared to me an imperfect solution but it was, I supposed, the only one available to him. He was no longer in Greece, able to stretch out on the beach, a bottle of olive oil perched beside him, and lie beneath the hot sun. Now it was my father's dirty laundry which lay beneath *him*. And up above, a layer of low grey clouds was depositing another pile of snow.

Leon had become pale since his arrival but, as compensation, his black head of hair and almost mordant-looking moustache had become darker, fiercer, as if a great winter wind was howling against him.

I'd concluded that he was a dangerous man, not to be discounted, but after his initial thrusts — the launch of my television set, the imposed family dinners — there'd been an unmistakable retreat. He'd been unable to counter my father's almost daily visitations and the strange effect they'd begun to have on my mother, who now sat patiently on the couch listening.

"Artists are shit converters," my father triumphantly declared. "Shit converters!" he repeated. "They feed off the fertile muck of life" — here he suddenly laughed — "and turn it into a rare, magnificent flower."

Was Leon a shit converter? Was that what he was doing upstairs? It took talent — a certain magic — to be a shit converter, I concluded, and the only one who could identify that magic, if not dispense it, was my father.

The triumphant sound of his voice suddenly vanished. "You're the muse, Aviva," he said quietly. Then, as if interrupting himself, he announced: "I've looked at Harriet's poems — they show an active imagination."

"Well, she's had a good teacher." There was a note of disappointment in my mother's voice.

"Yes," my father muttered, "she always showed up at class on time, she was a diligent student, studied hard, and was a good listener."

I felt a momentary sense of betrayal as I listened to my father. I'd only been to his university office once before and, apart from a bookshelf which supported oversized books, I remembered a plant in the corner which I'd found disquieting. Somehow, I'd been jealous of it. Though I couldn't imagine him ever noticing the plant, someone must have come every day to water its roots and tend to its leaves. I couldn't be sure if it was the plant or the person who cared for it which bothered me more, but its presence, so far from the house, was a hint of a life he was leading without me.

Harriet was more than a hint. She was, like me, a pupil subjected not to the peculiar habits of Mr. Mitchell but to those of my father. She must have laid eyes on my father's office plant many times before; for a moment I even imagined that she had been the one watering it.

"Harriet has talent, you know. Her poems show an active imagination," he repeated.

The news of Harriet's, as opposed to Leon's, talent failed to bring the same level of joy to my mother, but she listened nonetheless, inserting whenever she could her stubborn conviction that my father's happiness was all she cared for.

According to my father I also had certain talents, though in areas so vague I didn't even know they existed. "You're a sensualist, my boy," he called out to me one day. "It's a rare gift." I was deeply flattered to find that lying on a couch with my eyes closed was an activity deserving of my father's attention. Later, when I had my doubts, I asked him what a sensualist was.

"There are two types of people, David. Sensualists and materialists." On this last word my father's jaw stiffened as if he'd bitten into a hard, unripe pear. Clear which type he preferred, I walked away satisfied, but returned an hour later and asked him what the difference was.

"A sensualist is a man who enjoys the good things in life, while a materialist spends his whole life trying to acquire them." Sensing that I still wasn't a hundred percent clear on the distinction, he went on.

"You like Jacuzzis?"

I nodded.

"Of course you like Jacuzzis! You're a sensualist!" The word "Jacuzzi," coming from him, sounded ridiculously foreign and I laughed. I couldn't imagine my father plunging into its frothy, promising waters.

"Now, a materialist," my father went on, "finds no pleasure in the Jacuzzi itself, but in his ability to buy it." He looked at me as if to say, "Get it?"

"You enjoy the fruits of other people's labour." This, he let on, was a rather cunning move on my part, and he raised his hand in a mock toast.

Pleased, I left the room and wondered how I could further nourish my talent. Jacuzzis were too modest; Turkish baths came to mind but they seemed dank and a bit dangerous. A private jet, I thought. I saw myself sprawled out on the cabin floor, a pillow under my head, the sound of throbbing engines slowly putting me to sleep.

But certain doubts interrupted my imaginary slumber. If there were only sensualists and materialists in this world, which one was my father? It was clear from his distaste that he couldn't be a materialist. But a sensualist? My father counted his poems like Greek bank tellers counted money, licking his thumb every fifth or sixth poem. He lived off nobody's labour but his own, and yet, I could no more imagine him enjoying a Jacuzzi than wasting his time trying to acquire one.

I realized — too late — that my father had condemned me to one of two categories that he'd created and conveniently opted out of. This, I deduced, was *his* talent.

Leon's and Harriet's talents, from what I understood, were slightly different; they were closer to his own. And my mother existed in another, separate category altogether. He'd called her his muse, and in such a way that it sounded like a confession. He was up to something, I concluded. Something dangerous. And I wondered why my mother, who'd been placed in a far nobler category than my own, had failed to notice it.

The departure of my father usually heralded the arrival of Leon, who'd descend from the third-floor study an hour or so after my father had walked out the door. Leon still insisted we all eat together at the table, but this was no longer a matter of contention; our gathering for dinner had become routine and marked one of the few victories he could point to.

My mother could still ask, in moments of startling

irregularity, whether I'd washed my hands, and I could still tell her to fuck off, but Leon managed, though with increasing signs of fatigue, to insert his body between us; a great firewall that prevented the flames from catching.

As we sat down and waited for the supper which my mother, the muse, had prepared, Leon asked what books I'd been reading for English class. I told him we weren't reading anything for English class.

"You're reading poetry," my mother interrupted. "He's reading poetry," she said, this time to Leon. "You've always had a gift. He wrote several poems last year, it was impossible for him to sleep, you said you couldn't stop the words coming into your head." It was hard to know who my mother was talking to.

The poetry my mother referred to was actually one poem that Mr. Mitchell had commanded us to memorize and then recite before the entire class. I'd already failed my first rendition, having stalled after the second stanza, and had been feverishly pacing up and down my bedroom reciting out loud, when my mother had passed the door and offered me an indulgent smile.

Leon turned to look at me. "So you're a poet?"

"He's always shown talent," my mother said, coming to my defence.

He pounded the table with his fist. "Another genius!" he shouted.

Sensing that things were getting out of control, my mother immediately conveyed several dishes to the table in the hope that our mouths would become preoccupied with eating. She shoved a forkful of food into her mouth and cooed, "Mmmm."

But Leon was not about to take the bait.

"Perhaps David will join the dazzling pantheon of great Canadian writers."

My mother's reply was unexpected. "There is a tremendous amount of good Canadian literature, Leon."

"As there is Estonian."

"Yes, there probably is."

"Then all hail Estonia!" Leon thrust his right arm out, an act which disgusted my mother.

"In case you don't know it, we have writers who are famous all over the world."

"World famous in Canada," he shot back.

"I'm not going to have this argument with you."

"Listen, Aviva, no one's heard of Canadian literature outside of Toronto." "Toronto" was delivered in a scornful tone. "When I told my friends in London that I was moving to live with a Canadian woman and her adolescent son, they thought I was mad. 'Toronto?' they asked. I may as well have said Vladivostok."

"Toronto is hardly Vladivostok."

"No, perhaps not," he answered sensibly, "but if I ask you to picture it for me, what do you see? Snow, ice, maybe a few men drinking vodka. It's all vague. There's no information, no sense of the place."

These last words were, curiously, directed at me, and I found myself nodding in agreement. There *was* something vague about Toronto — something missing — otherwise why had my mother been in a constant state of house-mania? It was as if there were a gap between her teeth, and each new house another tooth she tried to wiggle into her mouth.

"I've travelled all over the world," said my mother, "and I can tell you that everyone knows Canada."

"What do you know of the world?"

My mother raised her hands and scoffed at Leon's question, an act which reminded me of my father.

"You've never lived anywhere. You've just been a tourist."

"I've lived in Greece for years!"

"Lived in Greece! Aviva! You go for the summer and leave as soon as it gets cold."

"Oh, as opposed to basking in the hot sun, which I do here." She looked pointedly at the frosted windowpanes behind her.

But Leon ignored her. "Do you think the Greeks have heard of Canadian literature?"

"That's not the point," my mother said wearily, but her fatigue was just an act.

"No, the point is you all arrive and let your tits hang out while the Greeks do their little summer dances before retreating back into their drafty tavernas." Leon pushed his chair back and stood up — "*Opa!*" he shouted, mimicking the Greek cry of delight.

"You have real problems," my mother answered.

"*Opa!*"

"'The Day Is Done,' by Henry Wadsworth Longfellow."

I held the sheet of paper which contained Longfellow's poem but, in accordance with Mr. Mitchell's edict, I placed it upon his wooden desk before launching into my recital. Mr. Mitchell was sitting in his chair and failed to look up.

> *"The day is done, and the darkness*
> *Falls from the wings of Night,*
> *As a feather is wafted downward*
> *From an eagle in his flight.*

"I see the lights of the village
Gleam through the rain and the mist,
And a feeling of sorrow comes o'er me
That my soul cannot resist:

"A feeling of sorrow and longing,
That is not akin to pain,
And resembles sorrow only
As the mist resembles the rain . . ."

Then I faltered.

I stood there for some time, searching for the words I knew were lodged somewhere in my head, but all that came to me was Leon's triumphant cry of "*Opa!*" I twirled the buttons of my shirt and waited to be dismissed.

Mr. Mitchell raised his head. "Try to remember."

I squeezed my eyes shut, but rather than remember the poem, my head exploded with images.

Opa! Opa! Opa! My father's hand was glued to a woman's leg.

Opa! Opa! Opa! Dania's foot was clenched in mine.

Opa! Opa! Opa! Katy's breasts swelled then collapsed on the carpeted floor of my private jet airplane.

Opa! Opa! Opa! Leon typed furiously in the study, pounding the floor with his feet.

Two chairs, a couch, and my mother's Moroccan beanbag deposited to one side of the fireplace constituted the seating arrangements of our living room. As I walked through the front door, Longfellow's poem stuffed into my front pocket, I found my mother scrutinizing the couches and chairs as if their arrangement could help explain her presence. She took no notice of me as I passed her in the hallway but remained trapped within the haphazard enclosure of chairs and beanbag.

Leon was sitting at the dining-room table, nibbling on several strips of cheese, but raised himself from his chair and sat down on the couch, looking at my mother in the same way she was looking at the furniture. They were both waiting for something.

"Hello, hello, hello!"

My father charged through the front door of the house like a bull from Pamplona.

"I have good news, Leon!"

My mother, having made herself catatonic in contemplation of the furniture, leaped to sudden attention.

"Would you like something to eat?"

Without waiting for a reply she dashed to the kitchen.

"Leon, I've just spoken to Tad Jaworski. He's a film director whose body of work has given him a solid reputation in Canada. He's received financing to make a film, a documentary, on Karl Marx. There's interest from the Canadians, the Germans, and the English. He approached me about writing the screenplay and I told him that I'm not the man for the job."

Just then my mother returned with an assortment of carrot and celery sticks, some of which jutted out of a thick, milky paste.

"Irving?" she asked.

This interruption annoyed my father, whose face momentarily darkened, but at her insistence he pulled a celery stalk out of its milky paste and jabbed it into his mouth like a picador. I looked over at my mother, who held the plate of vegetable lances in her hand. She needed to bleed him of his excess strength.

My father continued, "I told him I'm not the man

for this kind of work but I knew who was. 'Leon Whiteson,' I said, 'is a skilled writer and he needs work.'" My father bit into his celery stalk and eyed Leon with a look of paternal vengeance.

"It sounds interesting." Leon's long legs looked as if they were pushed up against an imaginary seat in front of him. He needed my private jet to stretch them out.

"He has financing!" This seemed to be important to my father. "There's money in it — twenty thousand dollars!"

"What would Marx have said to that?"

My father laughed; actually it was more of a howl. "A fool and his money, Leon. A fool and his money."

"Yes ..."

"Well? I told Tad Jaworski I'd give him an answer."

Without prompting, my mother said: "I think it's a very interesting project, Leon."

"Good, then I'll tell him."

My father, satisfied, walked to the front door and struggled with his overcoat; an angry negotiation. "Who makes these things?" The question was addressed to me. "If you buy a coat, make sure it doesn't have any sleeves or buttons." I shrugged in acknowledgment. Anything more exuberant might possibly reveal that he hadn't lived in the house for six months.

The dermatologist was located in the same building as the Ritalin doctor. I recognized the pharmacy. There was a possibility that I was to have my skin cleaned and my head cleared all in one day, but when I asked my mother she said I was mistaken; the doctor who prescribed the Ritalin was in another building.

My skin breakouts were becoming serious but the doctor, who touched several blemishes with a professional hand, was not alarmed. He'd seen far worse and told me so; he treated some patients with antibiotics.

There was very little alarm in my mother's face. She sat in the chair and looked on with a kind of mechanical interest, the same look she had when shopping for groceries. But despite her calm, the eruptions on my face, which had started in Greece as pinprick-sized blackheads, had evolved into fiery mounds which threatened me in ways I couldn't quite explain.

Although the dermatologist spoke of the "pathology" of pimples, their origin – the pimple's essence – was, by his own admission, unknown.

"He eats a lot of chocolate," my mother said. Then, because she felt this was too specific a crime, added, "He has a lot of sugar in his diet."

"There have been a number of studies looking into the relationship between diet and skin blemishes but so far, to be truthful, there hasn't been any significant correlation."

This answer annoyed my mother, but the doctor was firm.

"He has a sweet tooth," she reiterated.

The doctor shrugged in the same professional manner as he'd touched my pimples, and glanced in my direction as if to say he'd seen a hundred other mothers try to foist good eating habits upon their children.

"What about stress?" she persisted.

Yes. Stress. I still had the Longfellow poem in my pocket, in preparation for my next attempted recitation, and I'd begun to imagine that each word of the poem was lodged inside a pimple. One squeezed pimple meant one lost word. This fantasy, I thought, was a clear sign of stress.

Again, the doctor met this challenge with what

amounted to a shrug. Stress might have some bearing on the formation of pimples but then again it might not.

The doctor picked up a pen and made a quick, incisive scribble on a piece of paper which he then tore off the pad and handed to my mother. It was clear our meeting was coming to an end.

"This is a prescription," he said. "Take it downstairs to the pharmacy and they'll fill it out for you."

"Will it help him?"

"It'll alleviate some of the problems."

These were his final words.

I felt certain, entering the pharmacy, that it was the one which dispensed my Ritalin, but I kept this certainty to myself. I recognized the gaunt East Indian whose shabby white lab coat made him seem sadder than he probably was, standing behind a wall of vitamins and insoles. I'd watched him shepherd my pills with a plastic knife, silently counting each one with a flick of his tongue.

This time, instead of a vial of pills, I received a glass bottle filled with a dark, insidious-looking liquid. The instructions were clear: I was to shake the contents of the bottle vigorously and use the applicator to dab each pimple with this foul-smelling liquid.

Despite my urgent hope, I lacked confidence in the potion's power. How could a doctor who failed to understand the origin of this malady possibly prescribe its remedy? He was, as my father would say, a second-rater.

"'The Day Is Done,' by Henry Wadsworth Longfellow."

Mr. Mitchell was sitting at his desk but this time his lack of interest was more aggressive; he picked up a pen and began to mark papers.

*"The day is done, and the darkness
Falls from the wings of Night,
As a feather is wafted downward
From an eagle in his flight . . ."*

My mouth was like a caged door and, once it was opened, the words flew out of my mouth like a flock of common pigeons, entangled and startled by all the flapping wings. I hated this interest in words, their presumption of intelligence. I hated Mr. Mitchell. I hated Longfellow. They'd turned me into a fool, a keeper of pigeons.

*". . . And the night shall be filled with music,
And the cares, that infest the day,
Shall fold their tents, like the Arabs,
And as silently steal away."*

The end.

Nobody clapped. Nobody lifted me up on their shoulders and carried me out of the classroom. Mr. Mitchell, still marking papers, said: "Thank you."

As I went to sit down, Michael Chang, a recent immigrant from Hong Kong, took my place at the front of the class and mentioned the high-flying eagle before I'd been able to make myself comfortable in my chair.

Mercifully, Mr. Mitchell's class was the last of the day. It took only a few minutes to throw my books in a locker and head out the side doors.

"Jerusalem's the other way, mate."

Leon was leaning out of a car window. He honked. Several other cars were parked on the asphalt playing field, all in an orderly line except Leon's; he'd placed the nose of his car at a slight angle from the rest.

"What are you doing here?" I asked when I came close enough not to shout.

"The oranges," he answered.

The oranges. I'd forgotten all about them. I'd pleaded with Leon and my mother to buy a case of oranges several months back, stating their spectacular qualities — "They're not like the oranges you can buy in the store!" — and reminding them, as the school had instructed, to state that these oranges were for a worthy cause, though what that cause was, I hadn't the faintest idea.

"It's today?" I asked, but I was looking at the car.

"You like it?"

I didn't. It was the colour of a dusty fire engine, with a wide, long snout eagerly sniffing the cars parked in front. I was horrified, but Leon looked pleased with himself.

"It's from Rent-A-Wreck."

Leon reached out and handed me a ticket entitling us to one case of oranges, and then stepped out of the car. At some point I must have acclimatized to his appearance because now, away from the house, Leon, like the car, was a man who stood at odd angles from those around him. The blue jeans, the leather vest, the floral kerchief around his neck — he was a disturbing figure, my mother's very own Rent-A-Wreck: worn, sturdy, and strangely handsome.

The other cars, their tailpipes silently discharging exhaust, were better cared for but also heavier and more phlegmatic. Their sturdiness was of a different sort.

Leon and I collected our oranges from the school auditorium and placed the crate on the back seat of Leon's Rent-A-Wreck. Lawrence Weinstein walked past: "Nice car," he smirked.

"Better fucking shape than your pimples," Leon said. Then he ignited the car and sped out of the playground. When I looked out the back window I saw Lawrence Weinstein, looking shocked and wounded, fingering his face.

We hauled the crate of oranges into the house and pried it open. They *were* different than the ones found in the store. We each stuck a hand into the box and pulled out a swollen globe, pressing our nails into the flesh and ripping open the skin.

"They're rather obscene," Leon remarked.

We let the juice run down our hands and reached for another orange as soon as the first was eaten.

"Where's Mom?" I asked.

Leon said she was out shopping and would be back soon. We hovered over the crate and continued eating.

"I'm sorry," he said.

I looked at Leon. Not directly, but off to one side, wondering whether I should feign bewilderment.

"It's OK."

"Things have been a bit rough around here. You must be finding it quite difficult."

I licked the juice off my arm, a kind of nod.

"It's always been difficult around this house."

He laughed. "Yes, I know what you mean."

Leon offered me a J-Cloth from the kitchen sink.

"How's old Mr. Longfellow?"

I was shocked to hear his name, so soon after I'd abandoned him on Mr. Mitchell's desk.

"Dead as a doorknob?" he asked.

"I didn't do very well," I confessed.

"It's difficult to remember all the words. Did you study?"

This was a stunningly fair and practical question. Did I study? Was raising my fist in front of the bathroom mirror and commanding the image before me to weep in

adulation a form of study? Was kicking the wall in frustra-
tion a form of study?

"Sort of."

"You'll do better next time," Leon assured me. "It's
just a form of mimicry, like learning a language. If you
hear the words enough times it sticks in your head."

I asked if he spoke any languages.

"Two. Greek and Spanish. And English on my
good days."

"You speak Greek?"

"I lived there for three years. And Spain, with my
ex-wife and two children."

I found the news of Leon's children, and of his ex-
wife, strangely irrelevant. Standing before me, orange in
hand, he appeared totally committed to the present. His past
disturbed me far less than the plant in my father's office.

"You lived in Greece?"

"Not just Greece," Leon answered, "but in
Molyvos."

"I didn't know you lived in Molyvos."

"You thought you were the only one?"

I did. I'd seen him as the intruder. Now, for the
first time, I thought it might be the other way around.

"I'd like to live there," I said.

"It's a different place in winter. Dark and lonely
and cold. Then again, I might be talking about my marriage. I was writing a book and my fingers would freeze."
He raised his hand, wiggled several fingers, and added, "A
bad marriage is a negative apprenticeship."

This last statement had something to do with my
mother. I began to have the impression that everything
had to do with my mother, that he'd subjugated his
entire past, seeing it as nothing more than a path leading
towards her.

"I'd still want to live there," I said. "There" was away from "here," I thought. Away from Mr. Mitchell, from Longfellow, from this house, and everything in it. Dania and I would live in Stella's house and the winter winds would blow away the clutter: Nada, my mother, Brian the mime, Katy, all of them would be carried off, leaving Dania and me to spend our days and nights in solitude. Perhaps sensing my burgeoning fantasy, and the strange vacancy at its centre, Leon asked: "What do you want to be?"

His question was a savage intrusion.

"Nothing," I snapped.

"You want to be nothing?"

"I want to be a star!" I shouted.

Leon considered. "Well, how do you do that?"

"If you want to be a star you have to be a pig!"

"Well then," Leon said quietly, "you've got a really big problem."

"What's that?" I demanded.

"You're not a pig."

I retreated upstairs to my room, furious and ashamed.

Retreats of this sort usually led me in the opposite direction, towards the basement, but it was no longer a place to withdraw to. Ever since the destruction of the upstairs television, Leon and my mother came downstairs to watch news and the occasional movie. Even the furniture looked different; it had tightened. The seat cushions and cover slips, once sagging and rumpled, were crisp and orderly.

Ascension now marked my retreats, up to the second floor and my bedroom and then, several days later, still higher, to the third-floor study. The wooden stairs, painted a pale blue, drew me skyward, and I waited for

Leon to leave the house before making my ascent, careful
to place my foot on every step, counting them out as I'd
done when climbing the church steps of Petra with Dania.
There were far fewer steps leading to the study, but I still
managed to lose track, thinking how similar my own footsteps sounded to those of my father.

Some things were missing: my father's pipe-stand,
a bust of his head made of black clay. But everything else,
including a skull my mother had brought back from a
Greek cemetery years before, remained undisturbed, the
skull's blind gaze directed towards the great wooden desk,
my father's altar. It remained curiously unharmed; the
chair, typewriter, and desk lamp impatiently waiting for
an occupant. A colossal stapler also sat on the desk, daring
me to place my fingers into its gaping mouth.

The study felt far removed from the rest of the
house, even more so than the basement, which had the
weight of the house sitting on it. The attic windows looked
out over a canopy of trees where a few thin branches, bare
from winter, tapped against the panes of glass. The faint
moan of wind, followed by the sharp sound of tapping,
was the only sound up here. The mundane noises of the
house, of footsteps and clicking furnace, were unable to
infiltrate this upper sanctum as if, like cold air, such
sounds were unable to rise.

A number of books were scattered across the desk.
Several of them were opened, with dense, compressed lines
of print scarring the page; others were stacked in untidy
piles of two or three. But the book that grabbed my attention stood alone and unopened. A man with tousled hair
peered angrily from its cover, as if daring me to hit him,
but when I tried to step into his field of vision I noticed
that from whichever angle I chose, his eyes remained fixed
on distant objects. He demanded that I be ignored, and

that was as good a reason as any to want to hit him. The book's title was placed above his head, written in thick red letters, with a black outline: *Karl Marx.*

I jabbed my finger into the book and opened it up to a set of black-and-white photographs. On one side, a group of men angrily marched down a city street; on the other sat Karl Marx, his feet tucked beneath a desk, in an alarmingly cramped room cluttered with books and papers. Despite the differences, this was clearly a study, not unlike the one I now inhabited. And the man sitting at his desk: he looked like my father.

"Learning about the proletariat?"

Leon's voice frightened me. I jerked upward and spun around to face him, wondering why I hadn't heard him come up the stairs. He must have snuck up behind me. I'd promised myself to stay clear of Leon; now I was caught and unable to explain myself.

He pointed to the book I'd just been hovering over: "Do you know anything about Marx?"

I shook my head. "What did he do?"

Leon laughed. "That's a good question, and there are a lot of people who'd like an answer."

At Leon's suggestion I grabbed the desk chair, pulled it towards me, and sat down.

"I'm writing a screenplay about Marx."

I nodded. Tad Jaworski had come to the house several times and the two of them had sat on the couch, drinking copious amounts of coffee. My father had been right: they liked each other.

"He was a Communist, right?"

"Among other things," Leon answered.

Relieved that Leon hadn't made me account for my presence in the study and interested in the picture I'd just seen, I asked for a fuller explanation.

"It's difficult to explain, but Marx believed that the few should not have control over the many."

"Is that Communism?"

Leon sucked air into his lungs, a fierce inhalation that told me he was excited, and began to answer my question patiently, but his patience soon gave way to hurried words, as dense and compressed as the printed lines inside his books. "Injustice," "capitalism," "wealth," "working class." While his procession of words continued, I looked at the picture of Marx again, sitting in his chair, mired in a swamp of books and papers, and felt a growing fury towards him.

"He's stupid!" I shouted, interrupting Leon. "Does he actually think that everyone's the same? That everybody is going to live just like everybody else?" I waved my hand over Marx's face. "He's an idiot."

"Don't shoot the messenger." Leon tried to place a congenial grin on his face, but failed.

"You don't believe this stuff, do you? Some people," I said, tapping the top of my head with my finger, "are just smarter."

I looked once more at the photograph of Marx. He was one of them, I thought, a man who could ignore you even when looking at you. My father was here, in this room; he'd inserted himself through the cover of books. He was unstoppable, uncontrollable, a man who used the labour of others, including Leon's, including Marx's, for his own gain.

Shortly after, Leon banished my father from the house. The reasons for the banishment were somewhat in dispute but not the deed itself. Leon would no longer tolerate my father's presence in the house, and any such meeting would require some form of notification.

This "edict," as my mother disdainfully called it, would not be obeyed. Who did he think she was, a child? To which Leon answered: "If you're going to act like a child then you'll be treated like one." Oddly, this was the very posture my father was accused of taking and which now led to his banishment. He'd been dismissive of my mother while the three of them had been discussing a film, waving her words away like cigar smoke until Leon announced that nobody treated his woman like that, a statement he now repeated.

"Your woman?" my mother replied. "And anyway, who are you to tell me how anyone can speak to me? I can make those decisions myself."

But Leon refused to listen, speaking about some sort of emotional blindness, of vulgar dogs barking, the better, he said, to lure the sightless towards them.

The three of them had gone to the movies together, an activity my mother actively promoted: "We're good friends," she'd say to me, leaving me to wonder if that included all three of them — if the three points of the triangle were, as Mr. Mitchell liked to say, lined up — or if she was merely referring to her own sentiments. It was probably the latter, since Leon never left to see a film without coaxing and always returned in a mood far more damaged than before.

But this was the last time; he would no longer be ensnared by my mother's fantasies and he would no longer allow my father to do the same to her.

The anger in my mother's voice was tinged with incredulity. It was impossible, she reasoned, that her life had become so ludicrous that she was being told, at her age, whom she could and could not see. She attempted to stand firmly upon this principle when confronting Leon, but he countered that her life had always been ridiculous, that only now was she becoming aware of it, and therefore it was useless to blame him for being the one to point it out.

"You're asking me to state, for your own convenience, that my life has been ridiculous? Whatever you might think, Leon, my life has not been ridiculous and you are certainly not the one to make it less so. I've had a wonderful life," my mother said, raising her voice over Leon's objections, "and despite what you might think or accept, you wouldn't have been interested in me if I hadn't lived that life."

This enraged Leon, but my mother looked pleased with herself. She'd found a steady rock to stand on, one that was high enough for her to withstand Leon's fierce lashings: what is could only exist from what was, and the more Leon loved her, the more gratitude he should feel towards my father.

"Irving's lonely. He appreciates going out to the movies with us." This gentle plea, coming after her anger, had a measure of calculation about it, but she was pointing towards the wound that failed to heal: "I'm the one who left him, Leon. For you," she added. "I just can't bear to think of him alone."

"Without you, you mean. You can't bear to think of him without you."

Leon had heard these words before; they were the ones used to coax him out of the house and make him attend a movie, and I found them depressing. My father, charging through the front door, animated, gigantic, was a man who demanded supplication, not sympathy; otherwise, he began to look ridiculous and I found that unbearable.

This was my mother's fault; her sympathy made my

father look ridiculous. It was her way of getting back at him, for the ridiculous life he'd imposed upon her.

If Leon distrusted the sympathy shown by my mother to my father, he nevertheless succumbed, again and again, to her grievous logic.

I was grateful I hadn't joined them for that fateful jaunt to the movies; it was a family affair where one member of the family stayed behind. I couldn't remember the last time I'd gone to the movies with my mother and father — I even doubted that it had ever happened — but it was easy for me to picture what had angered Leon. I'd observed my father's gruff dismissals, but I'd also witnessed my mother's incessant chattering and I wasn't sure which angered Leon more. I could see her, sitting around a café table after the film, yammering on about "symbols" and "metaphors," about books she'd read.

I wasn't sure if my mother had always acted this way towards my father or if it was a recent development, but lately I'd become aware of her painful needs. She had desperate demands, demands only made, I noticed, upon my father, who evidently had the power to bestow upon her certain gifts found nowhere else. She wished to be noticed by my father's disinterested eye. Surely this was what pained Leon more than anything else; not my father's dismissal, but my mother's need of praise. I despised her for it.

Leon was going to break this bond between them, hold it up before them and then throw it down, like the television set, smashing it into a hundred pieces. I could see my father, confused, humiliated, and delighted at Leon's impassioned outburst. "But Leon, I don't know what you're talking about," he would have said, and then, turning to my mother as if to say, "Do you know what he's talking about?" he would have made a gracious, if hasty, departure.

My mother — the Muse — could only be a symbol,

she couldn't talk about one; when she tried, she wasn't worth listening to. My father, on the other hand, listened to Leon, had recognized him, and I couldn't fully understand why Leon withheld the one thing that my mother and I so desperately craved.

Despite my mother's adamant refusal to honour Leon's request, my father made no more visits to the house. Or, to be more precise, he made no more visits to the inside of the house. Conversation between the two of them was relegated to the front stoop and, when they wished to take a risk, the vestibule. Even with Leon out of the house, they dared go no further.

Leon tolerated my father's presence only on condition that he visit his son. I was the son. This fact was not wholly unfamiliar to me, but I had never heard it expressed so directly.

"I would never wish to damage your relationship with your father," Leon told me the day after he'd banished him from the house, but I felt that the damage had already been done — I'd begun to think of myself for the first time as my father's son. It was an unsatisfactory thought, one that I couldn't make much sense of. "He is my father, he is my father, he is my father," I repeated over and over again, squeezing my eyes shut, concentrating on the words. "He is my father." But it was like staring at myself in the mirror and trying to catch the whole of my face with my eyes.

It turned out that the man standing on the stoop, waiting to fetch his son, had certain obligations and I, in turn, had certain expectations; I felt embarrassed for both of us.

I'd learned to take time preparing myself for our excursions. He often held a mug of coffee in his hand, placed there by my mother, and they talked on the front stoop, not really caring if I put in an appearance.

"I'd invite you in," my mother would say.

"No, no, I wouldn't think of walking into my own house, perish the thought!" This was their routine and they seemed to enjoy it.

"In fact, Aviva, I'm in a generous mood today and I couldn't be more delighted."

While they talked I waited, wondering if I had a right to overhear their conversation. On his first visit I'd put my coat on and broiled in the living room, while the two of them kept talking. After that, I'd go downstairs to watch television. This day my mother must have been in a hurry, because she summoned me.

"David, your father is here to take you."

It was always like that: "to take you." Take me where, I wondered? Or was my father the actual destination?

We walked to Forest Hill Village, the place my mother once compared to a Grecian paradise, and sat down at the Ranch House restaurant, where we ordered a Coke and coffee. After our mostly silent walk, we put on a great display of bustle, grunting and sighing as we took off our coats and slid ourselves into the booth, while my father, in an extra burst of enthusiasm, flirted with the aged waitress who took our order.

"What a life," he exclaimed, and rubbed his hands together as if warming them in front of a fire. I repeated the words back to him, rubbing my own hands, which were cold and slightly clammy. After that we had very little to say. My father looked preoccupied.

"So, how's your mother?"

I said she was fine.

"Good," my father said. "Good."

Our Coke and coffee arrived, and to make conversation I asked why he drank coffee, which I found bitter and unpleasant. He didn't seem interested in the question so I watched him stir the mud-coloured liquid and then did the same with my Coke, using my straw as a spoon.

My father suddenly made an odd noise, a kind of throat snort which I took to be a rebuttal to a conversation going on in his head. He was far, far away. Then he took a sip of his coffee and placed the cup back on the table, avoiding the saucer.

"So how's Leon?" he asked.

I was formulating my answer when it occurred to me that his question was not about Leon and me, but simply Leon.

"He's fine."

"Good," my father said, and then added thoughtfully, "He's a good man. Good for your mother. A man with a future."

I looked down at my glass. A good man? Leon? The man who'd taken my mother from him, banished him from his own home. This, in my father's eyes, constituted a good man? He wished to shield me from his own impressions but there was more: I was certain that at the precise moment he uttered those words, he believed them to be true. "Leon is a good man." Moments later, or days later, he might say the opposite and he'd believe that too. These were his convictions: that he could shape the world with his own words and make of it whatever he wished it to be.

My father looked at his watch and said it was time to go. He paid the bill and we walked back up the road towards the house.

"Where's my car?"

"Isn't it at the house?"

But we'd now passed the house and his car wasn't there. I wondered why he hadn't parked it in the driveway or close by on the street, but I didn't bother to ask for fear I wouldn't receive an adequate answer.

We rounded the corner and scouted.

"Where'd you leave it?" I asked.

"Who knows?"

I ran up the street, then ran back and continued in the opposite direction.

"Dad," I shouted. "It's here."

He moved triumphantly towards me, pulling out the keys from his pocket.

"You should remember where you put things."

"You're so right, son. I don't know how I could lose sight of a damn car."

I didn't know either, but I wasn't surprised. He was a man who lost things; at least, this one time, I'd been able to help in the recovery.

Carrie's house was a few streets over from where my father had parked his car, and I decided to walk over and see if she was at home. She was in Mr. Mitchell's class and had found my Longfellow recital comic rather than tragic; I'd taken to going over and watching television with her. My father liked to say that every household is a foreign country, and I thought of his words as I walked through the front door and found the entire family huddled over a newly purchased clock-radio, in a kind of enthralled embrace. Carrie's older brother held the instruction manual in one hand and used the other to carefully calibrate the alarm dial, a look of intense concentration on his face.

We didn't have any clock-radios in our house, or anything else that I'd haphazardly stumbled upon in the homes of other people: electric carving knives, plug-in toothbrushes, blow-dryers, brothers or sisters. If it was true that all households were foreign countries, then what was mine?

After setting the alarm, Carrie's brother jerked his hand backwards as if he'd received a mild electric shock and waited, as we all did, for one of the small plastic shutters inside the clock-radio to flip over and push time ahead by one minute, triggering the alarm.

Over the exploding sound of music and static, Carrie's brother shouted: "You can set the alarm to either radio or electronic!" Then he tapped a button with his hand and all was quiet.

"That," he said, "is the snooze button."

We watched *Saturday Night Live* later in the evening, a show I hadn't even heard of until meeting Carrie. This was difficult to explain: how could I have watched so much television and never even heard of it? I sat on the couch with Carrie, her brother, and her mother, in a room that was comfortably cluttered and smelled of cheap food, and wondered at this oversight. It was as if my own television viewing were private, unconnected, and deeply disorganized.

I ate popcorn and Pop-Tarts and then went home. After the hysterical laughter on TV, followed by our own squeals, the empty streets on my way back home were eerily quiet; the only sound came from an occasional car gliding over wet pavement. Even my own breathing seemed muffled. It was the same inside my house; not a peaceful silence, just one provoked by a truce. Leon and my mother must have been upstairs in the bedroom, their door closed. The silence outdoors wasn't just mirrored inside the house, it emanated from here.

I went into my room, closed my door, and looked

around. I looked at my bed, my shelves, my desk, my lamp. There was something missing, something I desperately needed.

"That'll be $38.95."

The hardware store had several different clock-radios in stock and I'd chosen, as an act of self-restraint, the one displayed and priced in the middle. Still, $38.95 was a lot of money, more money by far than I'd ever spent before.

"Can you put it on my family's account?" It had to be asked just the right way, as a question whose answer I anticipated.

"Certainly."

The man pulled out a large ledger from behind the desk and worked his way through it, first by opening the book and flipping through several pages, then by dragging his finger down several columns until he found what he was looking for. The whole process lent a certain legitimacy to my enterprise; more than ever, I knew that my desire for a clock-radio was just.

There'd been no reason to ask either my mother or Leon, as they'd have said no, just as they'd said no to my request, made several months earlier, for a blow-dryer. The hardware store had blow-dryers as well. Lots of them. And electric carving knives. They had them because people bought them. My actions weren't only just, they were a measure of my sanity.

The clock-radio came in a large printed box which, after I'd signed the ledger, the man placed inside an over-sized plastic bag, holding the handles for me to slip my hands through.

"Thank you, and come again."

I said that I would.

There was only one small window looking into the Ranch House, which I passed on my way back home, and I looked in, expecting to find nothing but the memory of me and my father sitting in the booth, drinking our coffee and Coke. Instead, to my surprise, I found my mother and father, both talking, gesticulating wildly with their hands and laughing. Compared with the gloom that surrounded them and the strangulated conversation I'd had there not long ago, they seemed like two frantic hummingbirds.

I placed my clock-radio on the ground and pressed one eye against the windowpane. I had no fear of being detected; my parents were far too absorbed in each other to take any notice of a curious eyeball. But I felt as if it wasn't just my eyeball; it was also Leon's. I picked up my bag and hurried home.

"Where'd you get that clock-radio?"

Leon's question was addressed to me but my mother answered: "He bought it at the hardware store!"

They were both furious, but I was still amazed that I'd managed to hold on to the clock-radio for a whole day and night without detection; the alarm had woken me up that morning.

"How?"

"He used our credit account."

"You're going to take it back tomorrow!" Leon demanded.

"David, are you listening to us? Leon and I want you to take it back tomorrow."

"No!"

I hadn't expected my answer to be so direct. There
was a moment of silence before my mother said, "I don't
know why the hardware store allowed him to buy it."

"It doesn't matter," Leon answered. "David, you're
going to take it back."

"No! It's mine."

"It's not yours," Leon shouted back.

"Well, it's not yours either. The account's under
the name of Layton!" I looked at my mother, not for sympathy but as if to make an accusation — I saw you with Dad,
I know what you did and it isn't allowed.

"David," my mother said, "That's our account."

"It's *my* account."

Leon thrust his neck out. "I am not going to argue
with you."

"Good, I'm keeping it."

"You're not keeping it!"

"Fuck off!" I yelled. "Fuck off!" I ran upstairs and
slammed the door.

The clock-radio disappeared from my room two
days later, whisked away, I suspected, by my mother, but I
didn't feel deprived. Like a flash bulb, its radiant glow
remained behind. All I needed to do was blink my eyes.

I'd never been so aware of spring before. Previously,
there'd been only two seasons — winter and summer — and
the time between, when one season gradually slipped into
the other, had been of no consequence. It was already late
spring when I made its discovery, which came not from the
budding leaves and sprouting flowers — the signs of renewal
— but its opposite: my mother's deep, unflagging lethargy.
She'd taken to her bed and then, later, to the living-room

couch, her arm draped over her forehead. With the windows now open, the lush, humid scent of spring drifted over her prostrate body and into my nostrils.

I wondered if it had something to do with the clock-radio, since this object had marked the starting point of her decline, and I felt responsible. Watching her one afternoon as she lay on the couch sleeping, I became convinced that my desires had been the fatal blow. The frantic sound of chirping birds flooded through the open window, each one making a miniature demand — it was enough to knock my mother out cold. I wanted to kneel beside her and apologize: "I'm sorry for ever wanting the clock-radio, Mom, for making you take it back. I would have done it myself but I was embarrassed. They'd treated me so well at the hardware store, I didn't want to be humiliated pulling it out of its broken box. It's my fault and I won't do it again. I promise."

A loud knock on the front door interrupted my thoughts but barely made my mother flinch. I went to answer it.

"Hello, David. I hardly recognize you, you've grown so much."

The woman at the door gave a quick glance to a couple hovering behind her and then asked, "May we come in?"

I took half a step backward to let them through. When the woman caught sight of my mother she said, "It's nice to see you again, Mrs. Layton," but gave her a sharp look.

"Mrs. Layton" was still on the couch, though now awake and upright. She blinked.

"Your husband called last week about selling the house. Did he forget to tell you about the appointment?"

My mother began to straighten her clothes in

preparation for standing up – she looked as if she was brushing crumbs off her lap – but failed to answer.

Trying to be pleasant, the real estate agent smiled and said, "Your husband has such a wonderful British accent."

The agent and her two clients worked their way through the entire house, my mother manoeuvring herself out of the way, staying a step ahead of them, clearing up the dishes and clothes that lay scattered about the house. She was barely aware of her own activity and cleaned the house as she'd done her dress, as if it was littered with crumbs that needed to be brushed away. The real estate agent turned to the couple and said, "There's a wonderful study up here, very private. Of course you could convert it into a bedroom if you like."

Then they prepared to leave, thanking my mother, who eyed the sheets of paper they held in their hands with visible alarm. The sheets contained all the information about the house, its square footage, the height of its ceilings: it was the promissory note my mother had once held in her own hands and had given to me on my first visit to my father's attic. Now it was in the hands of other people – strangers – who carried it out the front door, flashing it before my mother's face as they waved goodbye. She hardly noticed when the real estate agent hammered the "For Sale" sign into our front lawn.

Over dinner that night Leon asked: "Did the real estate agent arrive this afternoon?"

"Yes."

"Good." Leon stuck a small potato into his mouth and sucked in some cold air.

"You could have told me, Leon. I didn't expect them."

"Even if I'd told you, you'd still not have expected

them." Struck by his gentle tone and her own doubts, she nodded.

"We had a plan, Aviva. I'd come for six months and then we'd move to London. It's time."

This was the first I'd heard of any plan, but if past experience was anything to go by, there was no reason to believe I shouldn't start packing my bags.

Chapter 5

SHOOT-UP HILL

"Hoi! We're going to give you ten seconds, right? And if you're still here, we're going to beat the shit out of you."

His hair was blue. That was the first thing I noticed. But this observation failed to take into account the weight of it, its density, its tremendous height. It rose like a mountain — an electric-blue mountain. Two friends stood beside him, lesser peaks, but no less threatening.

Still, it was hard to treat the matter seriously; I was leaning against the school wall with three other kids, the threat had been directed at all of us, not just me, it was recess, there were dozens of other students playing ball, talking, running, and there were teachers — adults — whose boredom lent them a comforting composure. And besides, the boy with the blue hair didn't seem particularly angry with us. He spoke of our imminent destruction as if it were a set of rigid rules which everyone, including himself, needed to follow.

I turned to the three people I'd been sharing a wall with, but they were gone; when I caught sight of them in the distance, their lightweight coats flapping furiously in the wind, it was clear they were running for their lives.

"Six, seven . . ."

Without concern for those getting away, without looking at me, the boy with the blue hair continued to count off on his fingers. Then I ran. It was late morning, with a few low clouds in the sky, but straight ahead of me was a wide open patch of blue. Summer blue. Everything else became a blur as I sped past the teachers and football players, the fences and brick walls of my new school. They'd been unable to save me. They were useless. Worse, they were hostile. Even the blue sky was hostile. And so I ran, faster than I'd ever run before, because it had become clear from the way the kid with the blue hair marked off his fingers that if he caught me he *would* beat the shit out of me.

Unsure of the rules, I spent the rest of the day in fear. Did hostilities cease after recess or was his threat permanent? Was it a particular wall, or wall-leaning in general that provoked him? After they'd run away, the three people I'd been sharing a wall with had disappeared. I remembered only one of their names: Trevor. He'd been in my last class before recess and, because he was the first one to talk to me at school, it was obvious he was at the low end of the social scale.

Though I appreciated the company, I harboured the strong conviction that if I was ever to succeed at this school I would have to get as far away from Trevor and his friends as possible. They'd all looked malnourished, and each possessed a distinct feature which aged their faces. With Trevor it was his chin. Long and bony, the skin darkened by subterranean hair, it pointed towards a shabby future and gave him a look of disappointment I'd never before experienced on a face my own age.

His chin was probably all I needed to know about what lay in store for me, and when the last class of the day ended I bolted out of my seat and headed for the school gates.

"Hey, mon, lend me ten pence?"

Trevor had warned me about the gatekeepers who stood at the front entrance and demanded an exit fee. They were from the "islands," though which islands I had not the faintest idea. Since they were black I thought of Mr. Mitchell and his stubborn walk to school and wondered if he'd left anything out of his story, like having to pay money every time he left for home.

I pushed a hand into my front pocket and wiggled my fingers in a frantic search for a ten-pence piece; I knew there wouldn't be any change if I pulled out a larger coin.

Seeing my struggle, the gatekeeper smiled: "Don't harm yourself." For a moment I thought he was going to rest his hand on my shoulder in an act of commiseration.

Despite my lack of confidence in the school's ability to ensure my safety, leaving its wide walled perimeter, after placing a ten-pence piece into the hands of the gatekeeper, induced panic. Nothing could save me now. I followed the stream of students flowing through the gates and down the street, and wondered if I should slip down a side street or stay with the crowd. Was there safety in numbers? Or would they all turn on me? Anything was possible. The crowd thinned after several blocks. I turned right, walked down a street narrower than the first, and when I was certain I wouldn't be detected, I made a sharp turn onto a small residential street composed of row houses with stunted garden walls made of brick. The sun was behind me, warming my back, a gentle hand pushing me forward.

Shoot-Up Hill. All the streets, like minor tribu-
taries, emptied onto this wide, angry road. There were
candy shops with sad smells, overhead railway tracks that
thundered in anger, vacant buildings and swastikas. It was
here that I looked for a taxi but, not finding one, I kept
walking for fear of standing still and marking myself as a
potential victim. Several of the street signs had been van-
dalized. Shoot-Up Hill. A crude drawing of a thick needle
turned the rectangular sign into a syringe casing. This was
not Forest Hill.

"Fifty-six Parliament Hill, Hampstead."

With these words the taxi, my magic carpet, sped
me home. Out on the street, I'd almost convinced myself
that those simple words, the verbal equivalent of ten pence,
weren't going to get me very far; I was going to need something more substantial to get out of here. I leaned back in
the cab and thought it impossible I'd ever return.

This was only the second time I remembered being
alone in a taxi — the first being that morning on my way to
school — and I was excited by the privacy. All it took was a
slam of the door for Shoot-Up Hill — all of London, in fact
— to be put at a careful distance. These taxis reminded me
of summers past, of Hamley's toy store, the London Zoo,
and Camden Market, when my mother and I had jumped
in and out of taxis just as we'd jumped in and out of
London, always on our way to somewhere else. Being alone
in my own taxi made me aware that things had changed,
pointed towards an unsettling permanence: I might be
jumping in and out of this cab, but I wasn't going anywhere.

I also realized that this might very well be my last
chance to take a taxi to and from school. At the end of my
street sat the train station. The trains left at a precise time;
my mother said that from now on I'd be catching the one
that left at 8:14 every morning.

I'd never seen blue hair before, and the fact that I'd first caught sight of it at my new school gave me cause for concern. My shirt was blue, too. Lacoste, made in France. I'd worn this very shirt to school in Toronto, and I suddenly remembered that when my mother had tried to slip a cheaper one past me, going so far as to switch labels, I'd howled and banged my head against the wall. I looked down at the alligator which sat directly over my left nipple. The open jaws looked as if they were about to bite it off.

Leon had lived in London before meeting my mother, and had now returned with what he spitefully called "extra baggage." If he laid claim to this baggage, the baggage evidently now made a claim of its own.

"After twenty-two years of marriage – a failed marriage – and two children, I was finally alone, a bachelor," he'd said once, then repeated it often, usually with a theatrical flourish. But it was not to last long – couldn't last long, Leon seemed to suggest. He wasn't built for such an existence, and after meeting my mother, he had not only acquired extra baggage, it appeared that he couldn't live without it.

A wide staircase led to the second floor and, behind the first door on the left, what my mother called "Leon's apartment." At one end of the room, facing the door, sat a wide, low bed with a wooden headboard squared against a corner; at the other end, a gigantic bay window overlooked the street. Spanning the room was an ornately decorated ceiling, cracked in places and stained, barely able to support the cheap light fixtures that dangled from its flaking ceiling. There had once been chandeliers in this room. Now there was Leon.

When I'd first walked into his apartment, placed my bags on the floor and sat on the edge of the bed, it had taken me almost an hour to realize that this room and Leon's apartment were one and the same. There were no other doors leading to other rooms, no blind corners. And no stairs leading to a third-floor attic. This was it.

"Luckily," as my mother put it, a Mr. de Barton, who lived down the hall, had dropped dead a few weeks earlier: I could take over his room. Past Leon's door, on the right, was the communal kitchen and past the kitchen, the bathroom. Another door on the left led to someone else's private room and at the far end, facing the hallway, was Mr. de Barton's.

Leon said that Mr. de Barton had fought in the war and collected lead soldiers. This last piece of information had been acquired only after his death, when Leon had entered his room and found them lined up against the wall in their hundreds. They were worth a lot of money, but no one had yet claimed them. The lead soldiers, like everything else of Mr. de Barton's, had been taken away and stored somewhere in London. There were no shelves on the walls, no chairs, no carpets, just a single bed, pushed against a wall, and a small night table with a lamp on top. These had been placed there by my mother, her gift of comfort, and there was nothing for me to do in this room but lie down on the bed and stare at the worn door handle whose varnish must have been rubbed off by Mr. de Barton's now lifeless hand.

A curtain and its metal rod tacked to the top of the window were the only other objects in the room. These, I suspected, belonged to Mr. de Barton though I couldn't be sure. They blocked out the afternoon light that came through the window. There was a garden below, which was forbidden to anyone except the tenants on the first floor.

Everything else in this house was shared, including the toilet and a pay phone bolted to a wall, where I often found my mother, a bowl full of coins in her hand, shouting into its mouthpiece as if on a long-distance call.

"David, are you there? Can I come in?"

"Yes."

"I didn't hear you come in," said my mother from behind the door, though I suspected she had. I watched the doorknob turn as it responded to my mother's hands. This was not my room but Mr. de Barton's and, out of respect and superstition, I reminded myself of this fact every time I reached for the doorknob.

My mother walked in and offered me an awkward smile. She always gave me this smile when coming into my empty room, as if constantly surprised by the dreary conditions she'd imposed upon me.

"How was your first day at school? Did you make any friends?"

I told her I almost got beat up.

"Well, there's nothing to worry about, things will get better." I suspected these were Leon's words, not her own, and that her flippancy was really an attempt to mask her concern.

"It's horrible there, Mom."

"It'll take some time to get used to it. I remember your first day of kindergarten. You were so scared you wouldn't let go of my hand."

"Mom, there are kids with blue hair and black kids who want money."

She sat down on the bed and, like me, stared at the door in front of her.

"Well, let's see how it goes for the next couple of weeks. If you want, you can take another taxi to school."

But this was not the answer I was looking for. I

turned away from the door and looked at her.

"Mom, please don't make me go back. Please!"

I knew that my mother had her doubts. A month before, and without much warning, she'd taken me to the wood-panelled offices of a private school, where we'd both sat down in red upholstered chairs and "chatted" with the headmaster, who was young and well dressed and assured us that he was always excited to have foreign students attend his school. But it turned out there were quite rigorous "requirements," one of which was skill in a foreign language. Which one would I like to test on? he asked. My mother joyously proclaimed that I spoke French though I didn't know a word, and shortly afterwards I followed an elderly man down a series of long hallways until we came to a large room with rows of wooden desks. He placed an exam booklet in front of me, handed me a pencil, and left without saying a word.

I flipped the pages to the language section — it was incomprehensible. Then I flipped to the mathematics section — it may as well have been in French. I was able to scribble some answers in the English section, but I wasn't at all sure they were correct. I put the pencil down and rubbed my sweating palms against my jeans. These were the wrong pants for this place; they had kneeholes. It occurred to me that students prepared for these sorts of tests, they didn't just walk in off the street, sit down, and giddily circle the subordinate clause of a given sentence. Or did they?

A row of metal-barred windows let some light into the room. I wouldn't be able to crawl out, but I could stand up, walk down the stairs, and exit through one of the side doors. It would be so simple; I'd be out in the open, anonymous, on a busy street and I could just keep walking until I grew tired. I felt that the rows of desks almost expected me to do it. They were empty now, but soon

they'd be filled with viciously bright kids who'd all passed
their tests. These desks were the accomplices to their
success and they had no time for the occasional idiot who
shuffled in off the street, taking a test he couldn't pass. I
didn't belong at this particular desk any more than I
belonged in Mr. de Barton's room. It wanted me to leave.

But I didn't. I sat there, waiting for the appropriate time it would have taken me to finish the exam; like
everything else, it was guesswork.

Without the elderly man to lead the way, I took my
time returning to the office, stopping in front of several
oil paintings: a man sitting on a horse, a vengeful expression on his face; another with a wide cape pinned against
his shoulders. When I entered the office my mother gave
me the same anxious smile she'd had when entering my
room, once again surprised by the circumstances in which
she'd placed her own son.

The headmaster took my exam sheet and placed it
on the desk. It would never be looked at. An understanding had developed between him and my mother while I'd
been away. Her clothes were no more appropriate than
mine, with her silver shoes bought at Camden Market, her
Moroccan silk shirt that billowed and sparkled without
even a puff of air. He liked my mother, however, and
found her interesting, even though she persisted in telling
him how interesting I was, how I had a "difficult" head
and had taken vast quantities of Ritalin to control it.
When we left, he shook her hand warmly and thanked us
for coming.

Out on the street my mother said: "Oh David, you
wouldn't want to go to this school anyway, it's all too stiff
and formal and they all have to wear school uniforms."

But I did. I desperately wanted to go to that school.
It would mean I'd passed the test.

"We'll eat early tonight," my mother said, getting up from the bed and walking towards the door. "And I'll make your favourite dinner." As I didn't have one I wondered what it could be.

We ate dinner in Leon's room, on a fold-out table sheathed in a green tablecloth. From the open door I could see my mother cooking food in the kitchen. A shadeless light bulb dangled from the ceiling. A square window overlooked a brick wall. Even if I had a favourite meal, I thought, it wouldn't come out of that place.

Still, for a brief moment it was possible to believe that this was all ours, Leon's room, the kitchen, the whole floor, maybe even the house, and that I could walk from room to room without fear of bumping into a stranger. This thought was obstructed, along with the view of my mother, by the sudden appearance of a man in the hallway who nodded at Leon, then continued on.

"There," my mother said pointedly as she placed a steak before me. "Meat is very expensive here."

When she returned with more food, my mother said, "People don't eat as much meat here as they do back home, which I think is healthy. In Australia they have meat for breakfast."

Leon picked up his knife and fork, making a series of quick incisions in his steak, then lifted a small, precisely cut piece up to his mouth: he had good table manners.

"David almost got beaten up today."

Leon laughed.

"I think it's serious."

"Leave your son alone. He doesn't need his mama worrying about him."

"Well, if I'm not going to worry about him, who is?"

"David knows what's best."

I knotted my brows and nodded, as if to show that my mother's concerns were not only unfounded, but unwanted.

After dinner, I followed my mother into the kitchen where she stood over a cavernous sink, wearing a pair of rubber gloves. A water heater, bolted to the wall, hissed and clicked with the turn of a tap and then exploded into life, its hot blue flames roaring in anger. There must have been a water heater in our house back home, but if so it was tucked away, hidden perhaps in the basement, a silent accomplice to our demands.

With the dishes done and put away in Leon's allotted cupboard, we retreated to his room, but there was very little to do; it was only a matter of time before I'd have to go to bed. I did everything I could to prolong my stay, asking questions when appropriate, or falling silent in the hope that they'd forget about me, but Leon never did. "Off to your room!" he ordered, pointing towards the hallway. Noticing my look of disappointment, he added, "You can't sleep with Mummy," which I thought was both unnecessary and cruel.

It was true though – I did want to sleep with my mother and Leon in his large bed. But I understood that it was more than impractical. I would have happily slept on a mattress spread out on the floor. Leon had stayed in my house in Toronto, and while I'd never slept in their bedroom, he used the rest of the house in perfect comfort, even taking over my father's study. I'd never begrudged him the right, though I questioned it, and somehow I felt hurt that he was incapable of returning the favour now that we were in London. Leon's apartment may have been composed of only one room, but it was his, just as the house back home was mine, and though Mr. de Barton's room was just down the hall, it was no one's home.

There were some compensations. While taking my shoes off and tucking them under my bed, I couldn't help noticing that the room had proportionately far more space than I'd been allotted back home. And it had a hardwood floor, something I knew my mother prized. She'd swept it that afternoon but a layer of dust, thick enough to leave tracks, still clung to the floor.

Seeing my fresh footprints, I was reminded of the corner grocery store in Forest Hill. The layer of sawdust, the meat counter; it had all excited my mother, offered her a promise I hadn't understood. Now the memory of that shop, with its stacks of food, its rows of meat, its pleasant faces . . . it all seemed like a beautiful dream.

My mother had been beside me that day. Just me and my mother. Leon didn't exist and my father never appeared. I was losing her, I thought. For all the time Leon had stayed at our house, it was only now that I realized he was taking her away from me.

I woke up with a burning stomach. It was as if the water heater had displaced itself and was now fuming inside my belly. I lay in bed hoping for the pain to subside, but the act of waiting only increased my discomfort until it became unbearable. I pulled my shoes out from under my bed and headed for Leon's room.

"Mom?"

I knocked on the door.

"David? What is it?"

"I have a stomach ache."

I heard a rustle of sheets and assumed it was my mother getting out of bed and coming to open the door, but it was Leon who stood before me in underwear and T-shirt. I backed away from the door, towards the kitchen, before my mother's concerned voice halted my retreat.

"What is it?" she asked again.

"My stomach. It really hurts." I tried to throw my words over Leon's broad shoulders by leaning back my head: the man was in my way.

"You look pale," Leon remarked and then stepped aside.

My mother was lying on the bed, her back propped up against the headboard. A faint depression in the mattress marked the spot where Leon had rested moments before, and though he now stood before me in his red underwear I imagined the spot still radiated the heat from his body; it was as if a part of him were still beside her, keeping a watchful eye.

"Owww!" I bent over in pain.

My mother jumped out of bed and searched for a thermometer. Normally she would have gone into the bathroom, but it was shared by others in the house and such particular essentials were now kept in Leon's room. The feeling that we were living in a hotel was enhanced when my mother pulled out of her bag the same thermometer — I recognized the white plastic case — she'd carried with her to Morocco and Greece and every other place she'd ever dragged me to.

She shook the mercury down.

"Put this in your mouth, under your tongue."

I lay on the bed, in the place my mother had just vacated. Beside me was Leon's mattress depression; if I rolled over I'd fall into it.

"You don't have a fever," she announced, pulling the thermometer out of my mouth and twirling it with her fingers. "Actually, it's slightly below normal."

"Maybe he has an under-fever." Leon's face pointed towards my mother but I felt his words were directed at me. It was a comment I didn't much appreciate.

My mother placed her hand on my forehead, her

fingers probing for any hidden discomfort, and let it rest there while she decided what to do.

The hospital was a few blocks from Leon's apartment. It was made of concrete and tinted glass and towered over the nearby stone buildings, which didn't so much surround it as cling to its sides, much as the houses of Molyvos did to its castle.

A great many buildings must have been levelled to make way for this building, a fact which filled me with pride as my mother and I approached the emergency entrance. I'd come to think of this modern hospital, which I'd passed several times before, as an emissary of Canada, and its smell of antiseptic efficiency immediately shut off the water heater that fumed inside my belly.

I was a little embarrassed, even discouraged, at this sudden reversal and felt it necessary to show an appropriate amount of pain, especially after I'd slipped into a blue medical gown and been escorted to a hospital bed.

My mother sat down beside me, on a small footstool she'd found in the corner, looking tired but peaceful. Perhaps she felt the same way about the hospital as I did, that it was a place where we could both rest in comfort, a respite from London and everything in it. Whatever the case, it wasn't until the doctor entered the room that she managed to lift herself up.

"I'm Dr. Proops. I've heard you've had some stomach trouble."

"I'm feeling OK," I said, which was a lie. I was feeling terrific.

"He's been in terrible pain," my mother interjected. "But I think he's feeling a bit better now."

"Good." Dr. Proops asked me several questions and then prodded my belly with his warm fingers. He appeared pleased with the results.

It was now late and I was ready to leave, but Dr. Proops asked me to roll over on my side. Then he snapped a rubber glove onto his hand and put a finger up my bum.

I should have found this particular action terribly unpleasant but instead I felt supremely satisfied. Despite my rapid recovery, Dr. Proops' examination ensured that I would not be returning to school the next day.

After my mother had tucked me into bed and left Mr. de Barton's room, I realized that I couldn't expect to receive a rectal from Dr. Proops every night. As a strategy for avoiding school it wasn't a very good one, but as a way to make Leon and my mother laugh it was remarkably successful. It was the first real laughter we'd shared since arriving in London and it became clear to me that I was here to stay. I thanked my stomach for giving me a one-day reprieve.

What I had taken as a measured account of our surroundings was, I soon found out, nothing but shock, and over the course of several weeks I watched it wear off until my mother's unhappiness was as bare as Mr. de Barton's door handle. "Favourite" meals were no longer served, and I often found her standing over the kitchen sink, a look of utter stupefaction on her face.

Whatever problems she might have had — and I suspected she had many — mine were just as consuming. My blue-haired tormenter, the one who'd threatened to destroy me on my first day of school, sat directly in front of me in history class. He wore a long silver earring which responded to every movement of his head and produced an unpleasantly hypnotic effect on me.

Miss Mallet, our teacher, was teaching something called the Industrial Revolution. She rattled off names and dates, spoke of the principles behind boiling kettles, steam engines, and water wheels. Cotton was mentioned and so were the Prussians. Every twenty minutes Miss Mallet would dash out for a fag break.

Leon's flat offered what I thought to be a possible example of the Industrial Revolution. The twenty-pound public telephone bolted to the wall, the water heaters and electrical outlets, all the things which back home were hidden and small were here exposed and gigantic as if they were made to service a world of destructive giants. This was the first explanation I'd been able to come up with since my arrival but it was, I knew, inadequate for understanding the course. Every few minutes the students would pick up their pens and write down a portion of the information Miss Mallet either uttered or scrawled on the blackboard and, while I mimicked their actions, I only managed to bring home cryptic scribblings that I was at a loss to decipher.

After the second week we were given a test, the announcement of which surprised no one but me. We were each given a blank sheet of paper and asked ten questions in rapid succession. Then we were asked to exchange these pieces of paper with our immediate neighbour and place a check mark beside each correct answer. My immediate neighbour was the boy with the blue hair. Even though I thought he looked fully prepared to rob a bank, my only fear now was that he would look at my test and laugh. Instead, when he handed back my paper with only two check marks compared with his perfect ten, he offered me a piece of stern advice: "You really need to study."

I was offered another piece of stern advice, though of a different sort, while pissing in the school bathroom shortly afterwards. This one came from Eli, who kicked me in the back and sent me sprawling into the long drainage urinal. When I picked myself up and shook the stars out of my head, I found Eli calmly washing his hands over the sink. His hair, cropped short, was dyed bright white, and when he'd finished washing his hands he ran them through his hair, back to front, as if he had a head of fur he wanted to thicken. Then he said goodbye and walked out the door.

When I told Julia Humphries, who sat beside me in math class, she warned me I should never expose my back to Eli. She called his compulsion to kick an "affectation."

Julia was, I thought, full of affectations herself. Thick dark lines rimmed her eyes and made them appear like those that peered out of Egyptian hieroglyphics. I wasn't sure if the girls in Forest Hill had ever worn makeup, but if they did it was nothing compared with what Julia smeared on her face.

As one of the most popular girls in school, she could afford to speak to a "Yankee" who still had a penchant for dual-control blow-dryers, and it was Julia who first filled me in on the different tribes that populated the school. The Bean Boys were the ones who stood at the school entrance and demanded a toll for passing, and the Punks, along with the Mohawks, a closely related subspecies, tended, so Julia said, to be of little danger unless I was a Mod and then, she informed me, I should be careful. The school had developed its own tribe called Trogs who, from what I could tell, assembled their outfits from bits and pieces of everyone else.

Then there was Eli and a few others like him. According to Julia, they belonged to no tribe at all.

Listening to her, I had the distinct impression that my physical well-being depended on this information, and I did my best to act the apt student, asking if there was a difference between shades of hair colour and wondering aloud what might happen if I refused to pay my exit toll. These were not simple questions and Julia did not offer simple answers. Hair colour, she informed me, was a matter of personal choice; it was a matter of sussing out what choice held the key to my own safety. As for paying ten pence at the gates, Julia had never paid a penny and promised to walk out with me after school to show me how it was done.

Her kindness, like Eli's viciousness, took me by surprise. I was living in a world of extremes, an adult world, where one could be flattered or flattened. I'd learned that attention of either sort could come at a moment's notice, hold me in its grasp like a lighthouse beam, and then, just as suddenly, sweep past, leaving me in darkness.

"Do you want to go back to Canada?"

My mother was leaning over the edge of the bed, frantically eyeing an open calendar that lay on the floor.

"Do you?"

She turned to look at me and gave me a wide, beatific smile that almost swallowed me whole.

"When?" I asked.

"Now," she answered. "Tonight."

"You mean it?"

"I've called Air Canada and we're leaving tonight."

With the mention of Air Canada, she reached for her address book and flipped open its pages which, in contrast to the calendar, were densely marked with names and numbers. Relieved by the sight of her own writing, she once again looked up at me.

"Pack your bags."

Leon, as if in sympathy with the grey day, stood motionless beside the bay window, staring at other bay windows across the street. His silent misery, more than my mother's command, confirmed that she was serious, and I raced towards Mr. de Barton's room to pack my bags, which had lain empty and crumpled in the corner closet since the day of my arrival.

There wasn't much to pack but it still took longer than I would have liked. When I finished I dragged the bags out into the hallway and marched into Leon's room without knocking. Not much had changed since I'd left; Leon was still standing beside the bay window, my mother was still sitting on the edge of the bed, but the focus of their attention had changed. The calendar had been pushed to one side, too far for my mother to reach. Leon was looking at the calendar.

"My bags are packed." Now it was my turn to offer a beatific smile.

I received a nod and no more. Perhaps I could have stood there indefinitely, waiting for my mother to take my hand and lead me out of the room, out of the house, and out of London, but instead I backed out into the hallway and stood patiently beside my bags. The hallway darkened as evening approached. I heard Leon's voice and then my mother's. The door was closed and I returned to my room, where I sat on the bed and waited.

It was a weekday. When we left that evening, I would be leaving not just London but also school; the thought filled me with such wonder and relief that I began to sing, tapping out the tune with my feet.

There was only one person I wished to call before I left: Dania. She went to the same school as I did, but for some reason I'd spoken to her only once and then just briefly, as we were making our way to different classrooms. She was a year behind me, one distinction among many that separated us. I'd hardly even recognized her when we'd met. Her hair, which had been long and straight, was now a mass of curls that haloed her head. It had managed to transform her face and I thought of her now as I did of the tenants in Leon's house — as a complete stranger who had inexplicably gained access to my private life.

As I waited to leave, and wondered what, if anything, I wanted to say to her, I thought of Duncan's remark that in Greece you could fall in love with a donkey, not because Dania reminded me of a donkey but because without Greece there was nothing remotely capable of joining us together. That's probably what Duncan had meant, and it explained what was happening behind the closed door. Leon had to work without Greece, against it even; if he let his guard down for even a moment, my mother's hair would curl in utter disregard for him.

I was in darkness now, still waiting for my mother to take me away. It was evening and I hadn't bothered to turn on the light. It seemed unnecessary to illuminate a room that I wouldn't see again or ever want to. My bags were waiting for me outside, in the hallway. Nothing of mine was in here except myself and perhaps the ghost of dead Mr. de Barton come to reclaim his lead soldiers.

Thinking it was time to push things along, I got up

to leave, but before I reached Leon's room I found my mother in the kitchen. *She was cooking.*

"Dinner won't be long."

I couldn't possibly come up with a suitable response and stood there, looking at her, wondering if there was any chance she might collapse into the sizzling frying pan and burn herself.

"Leon went out to see some friends." Here my mother mentioned their names for reasons I found inexplicable and then said: "So it's just you and me tonight."

I thought that was the point of my packed bags in the hallway, but my mother made no mention of them as we walked into Leon's room with plates of food in our hands. She couldn't have missed those bags since they were placed right beside the door, but apparently she did. I concluded that my mother was lost. It was the only explanation I could come up with. Not the normal kind of lost, when you can't recognize anything around you, but the kind where what's around you can't be seen.

The room had been tidied up since I'd left. The calendar had been put away and the bed made. The windowpanes were black from the night outside as if a dark curtain hung over them, and I realized that Leon had left some time ago and my mother had just let me sit in Mr. de Barton's room, fearing Eli and the Industrial Revolution. The thought infuriated me.

"Aren't we going to Canada?"

It would have been reasonable to expect my mother to sigh, to lay her knife and fork on the table, to offer an explanation. Even to shout in anger. I expected anything but the answer she gave me.

"No, not today," she said casually. I could have been asking if there was anything for dessert.

I pushed on.

"But what about the plane? The Air Canada plane? You said you'd booked the tickets. I even heard you book them over the phone." Which was partially true because I'd heard her speaking to someone on the downstairs telephone when I'd been sitting in my room.

"It left this afternoon." I didn't feel this piece of information was said with anything close to the appropriate sorrow it deserved and decided to do the mourning myself.

"This afternoon!" I wailed.

When I calmed down and resumed eating, I realized that "this afternoon" was a vague period of time upon which to have based my entire escape, and I began to wonder if there'd ever been the slightest possibility of catching the plane. My mother had ordered me to pack my bags at just about the time it was taking off from the airport.

If she had shown any sign of deceitfulness I might have been able to piece this all together and force her into a tearful confession but, as with the bags in the hallway, she was clearly oblivious to the mistakes she'd made.

After dinner my mother suggested I take a bath, and while she ran the water I picked up my bags and placed them back in Mr. de Barton's closet. The bathroom was on the other side of the wall and I could hear the stubborn click of the water heater followed by the menacing hiss after the gas ignited. Normally I didn't take a bath but preferred squatting, showering myself with the help of a rubber nozzle attached to the water faucets. Without a curtain, I had to push the nozzle close to my skin, to prevent water splashing onto the floor, but I was never entirely successful and wondered if others in the house had a better technique for washing themselves.

The bathtub was half a size larger than any I'd known back home. I felt dangerously submerged when I slipped into the water and kept my arms over the sides to steady myself. The walls were painted in the same failed colour as the kitchen and, as in the kitchen, there was a window overlooking some shit-brown bricks. It wasn't hard to imagine myself as a dirty dish soaking in the sink.

I knew that I was feeling sorry for myself but it was better than the fear which led to Dr. Proops. The fear would return, perhaps tonight, certainly within the week, and it would continue until I found a way out of here. My mother had given me hope, hope that her fears would alleviate my own, but here I was, soaking in dirty British water instead of on a plane streaking towards home.

Actually, as I stepped out of the water and pulled the plug I realized that I was the one who was dirty and not the water. Gazing at the black ring which surrounded the tub I noticed a can of cleanser and a sponge tucked beside one of the bathtub's legs. It must have been placed there by the previous occupant, who'd scrubbed the tub clean of his own dirt ring before leaving.

I realized that I'd never cleaned a bathtub before and had simply spent my life stepping out and walking away from my own dirt. The thought of my mother on her hands and knees, in this ugly room, diligently scrubbing away, brought tears to my eyes. Using my own hands and knees I leaned over to clean the tub myself. Why was she putting us both through this? Why! The previous misfortunes my mother had managed to place us in had always been temporary, but this time it was different. She couldn't get us out of this one. Something must have told her that however bad it was here, it was far worse back home, and this realization, more than the dirty bathtub, was what provoked my tears.

"Awright, David?"

Philip White, whose front left tooth had turned a shade of grey, smiled.

"Yeah," I answered, "I'm all right."

This was our little routine and it was a dangerous one because Philip, whose slicked-back hair and leather jacket marked him as a greaser, had very little, if any, interest in my well-being.

"Awright?" he asked again because our exchange wasn't yet over.

"Better than you, Philip."

I'd been standing in line waiting for my subsidized food of smelly meat, rhubarb, and custard, dreaming of Forest Hill, with its rows of chocolate bars and Coke machines, so spotless and pure that they struck me as almost honourable. They didn't have subsidized food in Forest Hill, unless one counted the salads and fresh fruits placed there on the insistence of parents. They certainly didn't have custard.

Philip made a habit of disturbing my dreams, and this made him perhaps the most dangerous person in school. I dreamed a lot and Philip was always there, waiting to pull me back.

Lately, there'd been an alarming escalation in our exchange. Philip would ask: "Awright, wanker?" And I'd echo back: "Yeah, I'm all right, wanker." Sometimes I'd mix it up and call him a shit-head, or a tool.

This was a very unhealthy way to respond to Philip. I tried to tell myself that I no longer cared about my safety, that I felt defeated and that my defeat was a liberation. I could do what I liked. This is what I told myself, but in truth I was scared shitless of Philip White. So what was I doing talking back to him, mimicking his accent? No one was more surprised than Philip. Quite possibly my actions would lead to disastrous consequences, but for now they offered me a protection of sorts. I incited laughter rather than fury, though when he exposed his rotten tooth I wondered how closely he allied one with the other.

"Look, a fireplace!"

My mother's house-mania, which had been transported across the Atlantic intact, shouldn't have taken me by surprise but, as with Philip White, I was no longer thinking straight, and I stood beside my mother, stunned that she should be pointing to a one-bar electric heater placed in the sealed hearth and calling it a fireplace.

Actually, house-mania was the wrong description for a place like London where houses, at least ones which didn't have five apartments in them, were out of the question. My mother's attention was focused on apartment buildings like this one, called Glenloch Court, which stretched half a block and was made of red brick stained black with age.

My mother and I were not alone in the apartment. The superintendent, who was stationed nearby, exuded an air of careless impatience that led me to believe he was capable of great violence. He'd shaved his head and the stubble, a kind of head beard which darkened his scalp, made him appear as if he were constantly leaning forward, waiting to knock out of the way anything which stood in front of him. He was no real estate agent.

My mother took me down a long, dim hallway where she presented me with my room. It was so dark, she needed to switch the light on in order to see it properly.

There was a large bed, high off the ground, covered in several layers of blankets.

"The whole place is furnished," my mother told me.

After I'd seen the other rooms I began to understand her enthusiasm for the "fireplace."

Desperate to leave the apartment, I tried to edge both of us out the door, but my mother wanted to show me the kitchen, which she enthused was "filled with light." This was true but unfortunate, because the walls and cupboards were a mustard yellow. The linoleum floor, out of sympathy, had yellowed as well.

The apartment was hideous, far worse than Leon's room, which compared with this place was spacious and grand, and it was even worse than Mr. de Barton's room, with its high ceilings and afternoon light. To my astonishment, I heard my mother ask the superintendent when we could move in.

"I need to do some work," he said.

He didn't seem to care whether we moved in today or never showed our faces again, but just as we were about to leave the building he turned to my mother and said, "You can move in two weeks from today," and shook my mother's hand.

Out on the street my mother acted as if she'd been blessed by a holy touch. She claimed that with just a little work it would be a wonderful home for us, a place of comfort.

"You'll have a real room," she said, "with your own bed and drawers." She was going to continue with her list of amenities but interrupted herself. "We're going to have our own kitchen and bathroom!"

It had been a steep and surprisingly swift fall. From Forest Hill, with its wall-to-wall carpets and breakfast nooks, to this: my mother in ecstasy because she no longer had to share the bathroom and kitchen with strangers. There was no doubt in my mind that she deserved this fall but I didn't think I deserved to fall down after her.

Still, Forest Hill had been a fall too, perhaps a much greater one. Where had my father been that day she'd showed me his study? I'd been the one to fill his absence, a little Irving who'd proclaimed that all was good and well.

Then, my mother's happiness had been dependent upon my father. Now, as she spoke of private bathrooms and sunlit kitchens, she seemed to think only of herself. Did Leon not need a third-floor study or did my mother think he didn't deserve one? Was this a victory for Leon or a terrible defeat? I couldn't tell.

I turned to look back at the building, which began at the fork of a road and then widened. It looked like a gigantic ocean liner, heading straight for us.

"Awright, David?"

Philip White was leaning over my desk, his palms pressed down on the graffiti-scarred wood like Mr. Mitchell's when he'd called me a "baby-boy." Normally, Philip's grey stump of a tooth would be exposed but this time he wasn't smiling.

"All right, Philip."

Hearing my words, Philip sucked in a great deal of air, leaned back, then blew it over the top of my head. Philip wasn't in my math class but he'd come into the room to make a special visit. Whatever was going to happen would take place in the next few minutes before the teacher's arrival. I glanced over at Julia, who widened her eyes, which could have been a sign of sympathy or a simple desire to ward me off.

Philip was staring at me.

"Listen David, I like you, right? But you see, I'm a bit crazy." He pointed an accusatory finger at himself and smiled. "I'm not right in the head sometimes. It just happens even if I don't want it to." Moved by his own suffering, Philip allowed his smile to collapse. "I don't want to hurt you, yeah, but I will if you don't stop taking the piss out of me. So just stay out of my way and if I catch you looking at me ... like I said, David, I like you."

As Philip passed the teacher on his way out of the classroom, one fear replaced another and I spent the next hour trying to understand number sequences on a logarithm chart. Julia leaned over after class.

"You need to be careful."

Philip's words had frightened me, but Julia's induced acute panic. In Forest Hill, I'd once dressed up as a greaser and lip-synched to a fifties song in a school play. Philip was far more accomplished; with his grey tooth, leather jacket, and slicked-back hair, he would have been a hit back home. Julia's warning reminded me that I wasn't back home.

"Early last year, Philip came to school and beat someone with a metal chain."

"You're kidding."

"No, David. It's true."

"But why? What did he do?"

"He nicked one of Philip's newspapers."

The answer made little sense to me.

"Philip sells papers," she explained. "To make money. One of his papers was nicked by someone in the school. I don't think he knew it was Philip selling those papers but Philip saw him run away. They had to take him to hospital."

"And Philip?" I asked.

"He was expelled for two months. Do you take the tube?"

"What?"

"Do you take the tube home?" Julia had closed her textbook and was placing it in her bag. I'd forgotten that math was the last class of the day. She was anxious to leave. "I want you to meet Fiona."

I followed Julia out through the school gates where we met Fiona, who was standing on the street, smoking a cigarette.

"Julia!" she shouted. "You dirty slag!" Fiona leaned over and pinched me. "You're a bit of awright."

I didn't take the tube home, but I hadn't had a chance to tell anybody so I followed Julia and Fiona to the station.

"Which train do you take?" Fiona asked me after we'd sat down on a platform bench, Julia and Fiona on either side of me.

"I don't know."

"Well, how do you get to school?"

"British Rail."

"Well, why are you here?"

I blushed.

Fiona pulled out a small bottle from her coat pocket, twisted off the cap, and handed it to me.

"You might need some of this."

Fiona and Julia quickly began to plot a route to take me home on the tube but their discussion was simply an attempt to give me a false sense of privacy. They were both smiling, waiting to see what I'd do with the bottle of booze.

"Have you ever drunk vodka?"

I vigorously asserted that I had.

"Well then," Fiona said, turning to Julia, "maybe Americans don't drink from mickeys."

"I'm Canadian," I protested.

Like Julia, Fiona had drawn dark circles around the lids of her eyes but whereas they made Julia's eyes beautiful, they made Fiona's appear captive and shrewd.

"Well, go on, drink," she said, squinting at me.

I put the bottle to my lips and sucked out a little of its clear liquid. I coughed wildly.

"We're having a party next week, do you want to come?" Julia asked.

I nodded and handed back the bottle.

The two of them talked and drank while I waited for the heat inside my throat and belly to dissolve.

"Do you think I need to be worried about Philip?"

"Don't worry about him," Julia said gently.

"But after what you told me ..."

Fiona found my anxiety boring if not disgraceful and cut me off.

"You'll be all right," she said impatiently.

This time I took a larger sip and coughed uncontrollably. Fiona placed a lighted cigarette between my lips.

"Try this."

Just then an express train blew past us, thrusting the smoke and vodka deep into my body. I floated off the ground and felt love for everyone, even Philip.

Leon's wink to me, as we stepped into our new apartment, was the only comment he made about our surroundings. I took it as acknowledgment that we were both at the mercy of my mother's obsessions and that it was best to lie low for a while. I felt secretly pleased that I'd been included in his tactical strategy. Actually, I experienced great relief just knowing there *was* a strategy. I'd begun to think otherwise, feeling that my life was ruled by the mindless instincts of others, but here was Leon with a plan, an objective. He was thinking. And that was good enough for me.

To celebrate our arrival, Leon and my mother threw a party. Food and particularly alcohol, which I scrutinized with new-found interest, weighed down the kitchen table, whose unsteady legs had been propped up with several magazines.

The apartment soon filled with smoke and laughter but it felt different than it had when my mother and I arrived at the beginning of summer. There were familiar faces: Nada of course was here — she'd been one of the first to arrive — and Katy and Paul. Even Dania's mother had come, accompanied by a dreadlocked Jamaican. But it was like being at a fairground off-season — the rides still twirled in the air, but it was cold outside and there were few visitors.

Joan was also at the party, and she approached me with a drink in hand.

"Oh, don't you look so sad," she said, bending down to greet me, though we were almost the same height. Her words were careless and mocking and had their effect: I wondered if it was my own mood which tainted the party. The problem was, I didn't feel sad. I was excited about my own upcoming party, the one Julia and Fiona had invited me to, and had snatched a bottle of Dubonnet from the kitchen table as preparation.

After Joan's comment I retreated to my room and opened the bottle of Dubonnet, which I'd hidden under the bed. I'd decided earlier on that evening to take gentle but frequent sips of the red liquid as a way of building up necessary tolerance. I was dimly aware that at the other party I'd be placing my body under great assault and I didn't want to spend my time choking on the alcoholic heat I'd experienced at the train platform.

"David?"

Nada didn't wait for an answer but had allowed me enough time to conceal whatever a boy of my age needed to conceal. After she swung open the door she said, "This is a big room," and, as if to prove her point, she walked around its perimeter until she reached the other side of my bed.

"Is Aviva happy here?" she asked.

Nada was very good at flattening out questions so they appeared plain and functional, but I found it odd she'd be asking me about my mother's state of mind.

"I think she likes it."

"And you, are you finding London any better?"

"Uh-huh."

Nada sat on the edge of my bed and smoothed a patch of blanket with her hand.

"It's so much fun to have the both of you here, so close." I'd seen little of Nada since we'd arrived in London, but I knew that during my days at school she and my mother often spent time together. Sometimes, my mother was still at the Hampstead coffee shop when I returned home. When she arrived with that familiar expression upon her face, a sort of vivacious fatigue, not unlike that of someone who'd just jogged a mile or so, I knew she'd been out with Nada.

"Have you spoken with your father?"

Nada's question struck me as outrageous. "No, I haven't spoken to him in a while."

"Well, when you do, tell Irving that I said hello."

With that, Nada lifted herself off the bed and left my room.

I reached for the bottle but learning how to drink was hard work and Nada had ruined my concentration.

Had I spoken to my father? What the fuck was she getting at? Of course I hadn't spoken with him. Nada knew that. Then again, maybe she didn't. Should I have spoken with him? Was I supposed to? How long had I been here?

My mother had spoken with him, I was sure. I'd never actually heard her and there weren't any obvious signs, as there were when she'd been out with Nada, but she'd spoken with him all the same. I just knew it. And I suppose there was nothing particularly wrong with this. Leon hadn't banished my father from the telephone, just from the house. Still, the thought of her talking to him seemed somewhat illicit, like when the two of them stood on the front stoop while Leon was out taking a walk.

I wondered if there was a part of Nada that wished Leon had kept on walking. When I thought back to the previous summer, I now recognized the disapproving face she'd worn when he was around.

"I didn't mean this to be permanent, Aviva." When had I heard Nada say this? Last summer in Molyvos? Back in London? I couldn't remember. Nada was more than just a collector of people, she also saw herself as the curator, arranging the pieces by theme and colour; obviously Leon had been part of a travelling exhibition, not a permanent installation. Whatever my parents' faults, Nada must have believed that Irving and Aviva belonged on the same wall, side by side. And she'd come to tell me that, out of a loyalty to my father that I, his son, didn't fully possess.

My father felt fictional at the best of times but here, in London, thousands of miles away, it hadn't even occurred to me that I should have spoken with him. He couldn't do anything. And if he could — if he did — it would be like Morocco. He'd appear out of nowhere and lead me to a better place.

According to Leon, my party was only a twenty-minute walk from where we lived, and after tracing the route in his *London A to Z* he wrote the directions down and handed them to me.

"Don't do anything I wouldn't do."

"Do you have money?" my mother asked anxiously.

"Why?" I answered. "So I can buy some friends?"

Seeing my mother blush, I turned to Leon and offered a more detailed accusation.

"When we first moved to Forest Hill, she offered me ten dollars for every new friend I brought to the house."

"Aviva!"

"It's true!" she wailed and covered her face with her hands. "I wanted him to have friends. To be happy."

Leon shook his head.

My mother rubbed her forehead with her fingers, as if wanting to rub out the memories.

"Can you ever forgive me? I must have been mad, I was certainly very unhappy. I didn't want you to be unhappy. That's my only defence."

"Christ, Aviva! Stop it!"

"Well, I did!" she protested. Then she tried to hand me some money.

"Put it away," Leon said.

Up until now we'd all been grinning like idiots — there is something wonderful about shame and stupidity — but my mother's face hardened.

"He should have his money. What if he needs to take a taxi home?"

"Put it away, Aviva," Leon repeated.

"You're so fucking stupid!" I shouted.

"Don't swear at your mother!" Leon shouted.

Things had become very ugly very quickly and Leon inserted his body between my mother and me.

"I'm not going to play policeman between the two of you." Real cop or not, Leon wore the uniform and we both looked to him for guidance.

Leon turned to me: "I'm on your side, but don't you ever talk to your mother like that again. If you want her to back off, come to me."

Leon jerked his head towards my mother.

"Back off, Aviva."

"Don't you ..."

He raised a finger; it reminded me of Dr. Proops.

"Bitch!" I whispered.

The three of us stood in the long dark hallway: Leon with his accusatory finger stuck in the air; my mother with her outstretched arm offering money; and me, directions clutched in hand. Slowly Leon backed away and then, without either one of us noticing, my mother reached out and fixed my collar.

"Have a great time."

"I will, Mom."

Just before I walked out the door, Leon tapped me on the shoulder and quietly placed a ten-pound note in my hand.

From the kitchen my mother shouted: "If you come home early, I'll make you something to eat."

I found it hard to believe that the party was only a twenty-minute walk away. A part of me resisted the thought that the characters who populated my school were neighbours, who wandered the same streets and frequented the same shops as my mother and me. They belonged to Shoot-Up Hill and roads equally nasty and exotic.

But Leon had been right. It was only a short walk away, down a series of residential streets, broken by occasional roundabouts with blinking yellow lights.

It was already crowded when I arrived and, not knowing anybody, I walked with false purpose through the apartment, hoping to find Julia and Fiona. Open doors led to a back garden, empty of people. I went outside and felt desperate, as if my skin lacked adhesion and wouldn't stick to anything.

The party was located on the first floor of a house which, like so many other houses in London, had been ruthlessly divided up into separate apartments. I'd learned from Nada that any place with a backyard was called a garden flat, which was a fancy way of describing an apartment that was unable to decide if it belonged to the first floor or the basement. But it was far nicer than Nada's flat and it had its own bathroom and kitchen, something I'd lately begun to appreciate.

In my hand I held the bottle of Dubonnet I'd snatched off the kitchen table. I'd meant to pass it to someone on my way into the party, or place it on a counter, but I was still holding on to it and wasn't sure if I should put it down or drink from it. It felt heavy and awkward, as if I were holding a dead bird.

When I looked back inside I saw Julia, who was talking with some people. Had she been there when I walked past, hidden by the crowd? Or had she seen me and let me pass her by? There was nothing for me to do out here in the garden, so I walked through the doors and stood beside her.

In Forest Hill people had hairstyles, hair that fluffed and flapped in the wind. Hair that was parted and divided. The hair here was altogether more serious. I'd already seen blue hair and hair that stood up on its hind legs — things I'd previously thought impossible — but now I noticed the opposite: hair that was perfectly possible, hair that did exactly what it was always meant to do, effortlessly.

Julia's arm slipped beneath mine.

"Have you spoken to Fiona?"

I shook my head.

"Then let's find her."

We'd only taken a few steps when Fiona staggered towards us. One eyelid drooped.

"Fiona, look who's here."

Fiona opened her mouth as if to speak but placed an oversized can of beer to her lips and gurgled.

At some point during the night, Fiona told me that the English lacked broad shoulders and that she'd like to move to Canada. She sat on my lap while my hand swirled around her breasts. She informed me that we were having a "snog." Fiona's warm body reminded me of summer heat, of Dania and Molyvos. After spending my nights in semi-nakedness with Dania, I'd returned to Canada and played spin the bottle in basement rec rooms. Once, when I'd reached over for my reward, I'd been slapped in the face.

The women in London were obviously different. Dania was from London and look how far I'd got with her. And now Fiona. I reached out for my Dubonnet, which had found its way back to me, and took a huge swig.

"Are you lads having a good time!"

Somebody shouted back, "Yes, Mrs. Kinnock," and turned up the music.

Mrs. Kinnock was leaning one hand against the door frame and using the other to hold on to a glass of wine. She was older than everyone else and wore a blue dress. A necklace made of large stones drooped down to her breasts.

"Don't!"

I'd managed to twirl several of Fiona's pubic hairs around my finger and was trying to push further down, beyond this hairy barrier.

"Don't, David!"

Fiona's voice lacked substance, as did the chair I was sitting on, the room I sat in, even the person seated on top of me; they'd been hollowed out. Fiona had been reduced to the patch of skin which touched my fingertips.

"Fuck off!"

Fiona pushed herself off me and grabbed her opened belt. "Rape!" she cried. "Rape!" When she resealed her pants, she staggered off towards the hallway, turned right, and disappeared.

Her charge seemed excessive. Maybe I'd gotten it wrong about girls in London? It was hard to say. It was hard to *think*. I felt at peace and then I felt sick. Though there was nothing in front of me, I seemed to push my way out to the garden where several people were bent over, vomiting. I joined them.

"Please, don't step in the flower beds."

This request came from a boy weaving anxiously around the bent-over bodies. He was younger than everyone else, by a year or two.

Somebody barked, "Fuck off, Kinnock."

I thought that Kinnock, whose party this was, and whose first name I didn't know, had a lot to be anxious about. There were pools of vomit in the garden, the television had been smashed, and as I made my way out the front door, I saw Mrs. Kinnock, his mother, snogging with Jonathan Summers — the boy with the blue hair.

"Do you want to go to Canada?"

My mother was at it again. It was hard to believe, but here she was, flushed with enthusiasm, asking if I'd like to return home.

"No, Mom, I'm OK. Why don't you go back and let me know how things are."

"I'm being serious."

"In that case I'll rush to my room and pack my bags."

It was a cold day and my mother was squatting in front of the bar heater — the "fireplace" — which might have explained her flushed face. She held her hands close to the grille for extra warmth.

Leon was sitting in one of the chairs by the window, seemingly impervious to the damp cold. I looked to him for assistance.

My mother turned to him: "Leon! Tell him."

"Tell him what?"

"About Canada!"

"Actually, I agree with David. I think you should go to Toronto and let us know how things are. David and I could do with the rest."

I offered to pack her bags.

"I'm not going," she said. "You are. To see your father."

The news took a long time to absorb; I was like a clump of soil, saturated from previous downpours, and it took a while for the words to sink in.

"You'll soon be off school for Christmas vacation." She rubbed her hands in front of the bar heater. "Your father's anxious to see you."

But not anxious to speak to me, I thought, because

I still hadn't had a chance to pass on Nada's message.

Leon and my mother left the house shortly after-
wards, to meet some friends and go shopping, and I
decided to have a bath. The last one I'd taken had been in
Leon's flat – the last day I'd supposedly been on my way to
Canada – and it was possible I equated one with the other.
Mention Canada, and I headed straight for hot water.

Admittedly, there were differences. Then, I'd
slipped into the bath as an act of consolation, a pale
reminder of the warmth and security of home. This time
I stepped into the bath to masturbate.

I'd been thinking about Julia quite a lot recently.
I couldn't imagine her ever screaming rape; she wasn't
one to raise her voice. On the other hand, I couldn't see
myself trying to shove my hands down her pants with quite
such force.

I was going to Canada! Maybe I'd take Julia with
me. The water flowed out of the faucet and spilled back
into the overflow drain. There wasn't any water heater
strapped to the wall, hissing at me, and the bathroom soon
filled with a white, pure mist – clouds from home.

When I stepped out of the bath, I heard the front
door rattling from a series of fierce, angry thumps. I
wrapped a towel around my waist, placed another one over
my shoulders, and headed down the hallway. Another
series of hard whacks reverberated through the apartment
before I managed to release the latch.

The superintendent, wrench in hand, stood before
me, his shaved head tilted pugnaciously forward. He eyed
the puffs of steam rising off my body with suspicion and
alarm. For a moment I thought he would lift the wrench
over my head and beat me senseless.

"I've been knocking on all the doors trying to find
out who's been using the hot water!"

I wanted to back away from the door but I was scared that the sight of my wet footprints on the carpeted floor would incite him to violence. I simply remained where I was, swathed in bath towels.

"There's a coal strike!" he screamed.

It was the first I'd heard of any coal strike. Coal, according to Miss Mallet, had fuelled the Industrial Revolution. Was it possible the superintendent was shovelling it into a blast furnace downstairs?

My incomprehension enraged him.

"Where are your parents?"

I told him they weren't here, they'd gone shopping.

"They're not here? Then what have you been doing? There's no water left!"

I hoped he wouldn't ponder this question too deeply and tried not to look guilty. It seemed I'd sucked out every last drop of hot water in the building. Worse, it had taken every last drop to recreate the pleasures of home. It was clear that London didn't provide enough energy for everybody to indulge their private fantasies.

"There's a coal strike!" the super shouted again. This time his tone was more pleading. And then, as if reading my thoughts, he added, "This is England!"

"How are you doing today? May I see your ticket?"

A narrow gap separated the platform from the aircraft, and as I stepped over it and looked down at the grey tarmac far below, I knew I was crossing the magic threshold.

I handed the steward my ticket and breathed in the delicious smell of jet fuel and disinfectant; the world of coal was now behind me.

"On the other side, halfway down the aircraft."

As the steward moved politely out of the way to let me pass and greeted the passenger behind me — "Good afternoon, Madam, may I see your ticket?" — I realized that if London was a place of giant machines, Canada was a land of giants. Everyone on the plane seemed enormous to me. And not just their bodies but their appetites. Trollies filled with tiny bottles of booze glided up and down the aisle. The stewardesses did nothing but push and pour, yet never managed to extinguish their passengers' needs. And then it was time for food. More trollies, more booze. Attention buttons dinged overhead, great bursts of laughter blew through the plane, bladders needed to be relieved; I was in the midst of some kind of organized riot, a world where everyone's desires could be easily accommodated. My father referred to these people as "Cunucks" and likened them to mules, lugging their small pleasures on their backs. He had weightier pleasures and even greater appetites than those who now surrounded me.

"Son!"

My father's call overwhelmed all the other voices raised in greeting. He waved — a gentle salute — and waited for me to plunge through the crowd towards him. Harriet stood beside him. She waved too.

I was surprised to see my father and then surprised by my surprise. As usual, I'd been poorly informed. I'd not been told when the plane would arrive, who would greet me, or where I'd be taken, but this could not adequately explain the shock I experienced at seeing my father. I'd come to visit him, and here he was.

"It's good to see you, son."

"Welcome home," Harriet added, smiling.

"You look almost handsome, a real man. You see, Harriet? I know how to make them."

In the car, as we made our way along the cold roads, my father asked about London, my mother, Leon, even school. I passed on Nada's message, which touched him: "Ah, Nada," he said. "She always danced to her own tune."

Harriet, who was driving, pulled up to a recently plowed driveway, edged forward, and then turned off the engine.

"Home," she said.

Harriet showed me to my room on the second floor, explaining that it was her brother's but that he was out of town. I saw a picture of him, beside his bed. Another one, on top of a clothes cabinet, also included Harriet and their parents.

"Home," in this case, didn't mean the place where my father lived. Or Harriet, for that matter. This house belonged to her parents. It was a family home, a deeper home, that took in strangers like my father, even my father's children, and made them their own. I don't think my father had ever belonged to this type of home before and I wondered how he was coping.

Harriet left me to unpack, but I chose to lie on the bed and stare at the floor, which was covered in wall-to-wall carpeting. I'd come to think of this particular piece of decor as a Canadian invention — in my mother's eyes it rivalled the steam engine — and I wondered whose feet now touched the carpets of our old home. It occurred to me that my father, who'd never shown any interest in Forest Hill, had arrived at a home my mother could only have dreamed about.

I heard the front door open and close several times, accompanied by loud greetings similar to those at the airport, and then listened to several pairs of footsteps pass by. More doors opened and closed. I kept staring at the carpeted floor though I'd long ago lost interest in it. Then my door swung open and my father poked his head through.

"Dinner, son." He sounded hurried and I quickly followed him down the steps to the dining room where Harriet's parents and grandparents sat at their chairs, ready to eat. I was informally introduced to everyone around the table and formally welcomed by Harriet's mother, but it was Harriet's father who held my interest. He, and not my father, sat at the head of the table. He was younger than my father.

"So you live in London?" he asked, shortly after we'd started eating. He mentioned that he'd recently been to England and that, to his mind, it was slipping into penury. Excluding my masturbatory session, I told him my story about the bath and the coal strike, saw him shake his head in agreement, and immediately felt as if I was betraying a confidence. This house was heavy with furniture and food, and my lips were already becoming chapped from the dry, hot air. It felt as if a dragon was downstairs, blowing fire through the air vents.

My father was busy eating his meat and vegetables. He'd put on weight. His forearms, which I'd always remembered as being thick and hairy, reaching out to the world as if to strangle it, had shrunk and become nothing more than appendages to his expanding body. But even as his body had grown, his presence, like his forearms, had diminished. When he was silent, conversation flowed past him. When he spoke, no one froze to attention.

I didn't know what I had against this family — they'd been nice enough — but I wished, craved, that my father would suddenly stand up and rain thunderous destruction upon their heads, smite them down, and leave nothing but smoking ruins behind. I was certain my father was capable of this; somehow he'd become disarmed and these people were responsible.

When I woke the next day, my bottom lip had cracked in three places. It felt as if the furnace dragon had blown fire right down my throat. I looked out the window. Snow and ice. After putting on a T-shirt and a pair of pants I walked downstairs to get something to drink, but two maids, in uniform, were cleaning up the kitchen before the rest of the household had awakened. The maids took me by surprise and I retreated to my room. Needing to escape, I also needed somewhere to escape to. I quietly stepped back down the stairs, put on my winter coat, and walked to my former house.

It didn't take long. I stood on the sidewalk, in front of my home, and squinted. My memories were fragmentary, jumbled, and without order. I kicked Foxy Lady in the ass, heard my mother's wail as the plaster fell off the ceiling, placed my toes on the plush bedroom carpet. I had only one coherent memory and it wasn't even mine. It was Leon's, standing before the house one winter's day, wondering how these snowy wastes contained all his passion.

I raised my head and peered up at the study window.

I'd used Leon's eyes before but they'd never felt as strong or focused as they did now. It explained how everything could look the same but be utterly different. I thought of Glenloch Court — the brick ocean liner. Its wake alone would have capsized these houses instantly.

Leon must have known that. He'd walked into an overheated home, cluttered with unhappiness. There was a hysterical woman, a man who brought in dirty laundry, and a little boy high on Ritalin, farting on his bed and watching television.

I was driven to Montreal the next day. My father no longer lived in Toronto but had moved some time ago. It was news to me and, like most news, I'd been forced to read about it in somebody else's paper. Harriet did the driving — it was her car — and shortly after leaving the out- skirts of the city I asked why he'd moved. My father answered that he never felt at home in Toronto. He called it sterile.

"What do you think?" he asked, turning his head.

I thought there'd been just a little too much com- motion in Toronto to consider it sterile, but there was something in what my father was saying, something about those houses in Forest Hill, which needed to be described. I said that Toronto didn't seem to have a soul.

"You hear that, he says it doesn't have a soul!"

This remark was presumably directed towards Harriet, but he hadn't mentioned her by name and she continued to drive without answering.

"Montreal has character. A face. You can't say that about Toronto. But the city was good to me, I can't com- plain. Aviva and I had some wonderful times there."

Although I wasn't looking at Harriet, I acted as if I was and turned away. I wasn't sure if the mention of my mother would upset her and I didn't want to find out.

I quickly asked him about other places. Greeks, he said, were sneaky and Romans were like cats who purred when you were there and forgot about you when you weren't. He admired them.

"But I was born in Montreal and I spent most of my life there. You were born there too, remember?"

My father turned back around and gazed out the

front window. Was he trying to piece things together, much as I had tried to do when standing outside my old house in Forest Hill? Was it all a jumble for him or was there cohesion? One thing was certain: after my mother left, Montreal became his home. In Toronto, my father no longer sat at the head of the table.

Harriet and my father lived in an apartment in the centre of Montreal. I'd come to believe that nobody in Canada lived in an apartment and felt disappointed.

"Home!" my father proclaimed and made a dash for the study. Harriet made a perfunctory stop at my room and then headed to the other side of the apartment. I was in the middle, but I was no mediator in the conflict which had broken out between them and I waited in my room for things to blow over.

Ben's Delicatessen was responsible for the present mood. The Montreal smoked-meat sandwiches hadn't pleased her and she'd stuck to a wilted salad while my father and I shoved great quantities of food down our throats.

"The best sandwiches in town," my father had gleefully announced, but he'd known he was in trouble and had kept his head down, picking with his fingers the meat which had fallen onto his plate. Ben's was not a proper restaurant, it was a deli, and a rather depressing one, its yellow walls adorned with black-and-white photos of movie stars and hockey players. Harriet, after the long drive, had wanted to go to a proper restaurant. She'd been very clear on this point.

"You don't have to eat sandwiches!" my father had said in the car. "It's a restaurant. They have a menu."

"It's not a restaurant! And I've been driving all day and I want to go eat something good."

"What's wrong with Ben's!" Then my father very incautiously turned to me and said: "David, don't you want a good Montreal smoked-meat sandwich?"

I muttered that it didn't matter to me, an answer that satisfied no one.

"Fine, Irving. You want to go to Ben's, we'll go to Ben's."

The remainder of the drive had been taken in silence. Harriet listened to the radio, a pop station with commercial jingles. My father tapped out the tunes with his fingers, a sight that horrified me.

Thanks to Ben's, I wouldn't be called in for dinner or anything else that evening, and I picked up my little toilet kit — a gift from my mother — and walked into the bathroom to prepare for bed. That's when I saw the bathtub. In truth, I shouldn't really have been so surprised at what I found. The signs were all there: Harriet's desire for a "proper" restaurant, so close to my mother's desire for a "proper" house; my father's ready incomprehension and quick dash to the study. We were in the midst of hurricane season and it was clear that it wouldn't blow over any time soon.

I leaned over the bathtub. My symbol for Canada, for everything clean and warm, was ringed with a thick layer of dirt.

Irving and Harriet were locked in an ugly, protracted battle whose front was the bathtub. She refused to clean up my father's dirt and my father, rather easily I imagined, refused to acknowledge his mess. He stepped into the bathtub each day and added a new layer of hairy grime. Then he stepped out and wrote poetry.

Harriet had shown me a good measure of kindness but she was not my mother and I could expect little from her. I spent my days playing video games on St. Catherine Street with the pocket money my mother had given me before I left London. In the late afternoon, I'd return to the apartment and read about Roman emperors. One of the emperors, Tiberius, liked to swim naked in his pool while little boys nibbled away on his fleshy skin. According to the book, which I'd found in the living room, their teeth had been pulled out.

On my last night, Harriet placed a chunk of corned beef on the table.

"Ohhh, corned beef!" My father rubbed his hands together. "What's the occasion, my love?"

"It's your son's last evening, Irving."

"Really? Well, David, we should have more last evenings together."

Harriet plunged an oversized fork into the beef and carved.

"So, what are you reading?"

"*The Roman Emperors.*"

"You're reading about the emperors? Have you got to Caligula? He was very cruel." My father smiled in delight as Harriet placed a large slab of meat on his plate.

I told him about Tiberius and the little boys who nibbled. "Yes, yes," he cried.

I curled my lips around my teeth and bit the air.

"A toast to my wonderful son who reads about the Romans. You've delighted us with your presence." My father raised his arms as if in victory and then began to eat. Harriet placed a bowl of coleslaw in front of me.

"Do you remember Suzanne?" I asked.

"Who?"

"Suzanne. She had long black hair. Lived with Leonard."

"Of course. She was very beautiful. Made Leonard miserable. What about her?"

"I remember she wanted to file down her two front teeth. It's one of the few memories I have of Montreal."

"Really?" My father raised his eyebrows but I could tell he wasn't very interested.

"I was with Mom in a coffee shop. It was summertime and Suzanne thought her front teeth were too long. She even showed me, which is why I think I still remember."

"What did your mother think?"

This question came from Harriet, who'd just sat down at the table.

"I think my mother said she was beautiful and didn't need to file her teeth down, that they gave her character, but Suzanne said they weren't perfect and she wanted them to be perfect."

"That's Suzanne for you," my father said. "Never could find it in herself to be happy. Naturally, this is what attracted Leonard. Have you read any of his books or poems? I have them, you know."

I hadn't read any of Leonard's books or poems and I clearly sensed that I didn't want to. I thought back to the summer my father had rejected me for Leonard and left me behind with my mother. I wasn't a "woman's man," as my father called Leonard, I was my mother's boy. Even now, I was interested only in what bored my father. I remembered Suzanne and her teeth, not Leonard and his poems. I would never provide a home for my father, a refuge from Harriet, my mother, or anyone else who disturbed his thoughts. After all, I was part of the disturbance. And even then a minor one.

"I'm leaving tomorrow."

"So you are. You should read him. Another Montreal boy. A city with character makes characters." Delighted with his joke, my father polished off the rest of his food.

"More, Irving?" Harriet lifted up the carving knife.

"More?" My father managed to sound alarmed. I was alarmed. He'd eaten a great deal and the extra weight was causing him to breathe deeply.

Harriet grabbed hold of the fork handle and carved an enormously thick slab of beef. She placed it before him.

"Here you go."

My father gasped for air and then swooped down on his meat.

My flight back to London arrived early in the morning and Leon was there to meet me. To my surprise, he'd come by car, a Citroën 2CV, whose gearshift protruded from the dashboard. It caused him problems on the way out of the airport but once on the highway he let go of the handle and relaxed.

"How's your father?"

We passed some large brick buildings, empty factories with missing windows.

"Sometimes I feel he's inside me."

"Children often feel that way about their parents. A kind of haunting of the bowels. But don't worry, he's not there. I promise."

"I didn't say I was worried."

The 2CV was like a water heater on wheels. It hissed and rattled. Each time Leon pulled the gearshift I feared he'd take the dashboard with him. England wasn't full of large machines any more. At some point they'd shrunk.

"David, your mother went to Australia a few days ago. I'm sorry to tell you this but your grandmother died while you were away. Aviva was very upset."

"When did she leave?"

"Only a few days ago. We were going to send you an air ticket to join her."

I'd become accustomed to promised air tickets that never materialized and didn't push for an explanation, but I wondered what the distance was between Toronto and Sydney. Was I closer to her now or farther away? Leon could have made the calculation for me but he looked exhausted, as if the properties of the car — underpowered and shaky — had managed to transfer themselves to him. "Anyway," he said, turning to me, "it'll give us some time to spend alone."

Leon had rented a television, which sat on wheels in the living room. We watched a tennis tournament played in the United States. It was sunny there every day, the clay court shone like a swimming pool, and women rested beneath white umbrellas. The television was a bright little window, far better than the one looking out over our dour street in London. We ate food and compared players.

On the day of the women's semifinals, Leon said, "Your mother betrayed me."

I kept my eyes on the ball while Leon left the room and returned with a stack of letters, secured with a rubber band.

"She's been writing to your father."

Out of pride, even a sense of justice, Leon had wielded his influence to protect me from the affairs of my parents — even from *his* affairs with my parents. He must have been in great pain, even desperate. I sympathized, but he'd broken his own rules and I resented him for it.

"There's nothing wrong with a few letters." I looked at the stack; it was more than a few.

"She wants to try and work things out with Irving. I'm an interlude."

The proof must have been in the letters she'd sent him, but how had they ended up in Leon's hands? If he'd intercepted them, perhaps following her to the postbox, I was dealing with a man whose passions had flared too brightly.

Detecting my concern, he pointed to the postage stamps.

"Look, it says 'Return to Sender.' Aviva's been writing to Irving for months but she reversed the last two numbers of his street address." Leon widened his eyes. It was clear he attached great significance to this mistake.

"I've asked your mother to marry me. Twice."

"My mother's an idiot but she'll end up doing the right thing. After all, she's a Layton." I'd meant this to refer to myself but saw my mistake. "Well, you know what I mean," I quickly added.

"Yes, I do," he answered, laughing at my error. Then he stopped laughing. "You know, David, you're a bastard."

"Thank you very much." I pretended to be indignant.

"You know what I mean, don't you?"

I nodded but it became clear that I'd missed something.

"Your mother and father never got married."

"But what about my mother's ring?"

"It's Leonard's ring," Leon answered.

"My mother's married to Leonard?"

"He bought her the ring — the wedding ring."

Leon placed the bundle of letters on the floor and

gave an angry sigh. "Your father agreed to marry your mother years ago, and the two of them invited Leonard to come and celebrate the news. Later that day they marched down to a jewellery shop so Irving could pick out a ring. He bought a bracelet instead — for another woman — and then walked out of the store. It was Leonard who bought her the ring out of sympathy. I think of that ring as a kind of bandage, covering a wound."

I thought there would be trouble between Leon and my mother when she arrived back from Australia but their two wounds cancelled each other out; they respected each other's bandages and when they came off we no longer lived at Glenloch Court but had moved back to Parliament Hill, in a house that stood directly next door to Leon's old flat.

It was a garden flat with a real fireplace. I was given two rooms, a bedroom and a small study, where I spent an hour each evening doing my homework. Leon also had a study, and he resumed his work on Marx, mostly during the day while I was at school, but occasionally at night, while I was studying. Afterwards, we'd all gather in the living room, whose doors opened directly on the back garden, to talk and watch television.

My grandmother had made this move possible. She'd left a small sum of money, and it was being put towards the rent of our new flat. This was her legacy, given to my mother. But it was my gift too. She was the last grandparent I had — the only one I'd known — and it had been her wish that all of us, including Leon, though I had no real proof of this, live in a garden flat.

Perhaps sensing the advantage provided by my

grandmother, Leon asked, once again, for my mother's hand in marriage. She responded by taking me to Venice. She said the city represented decay and decadence, and we walked happily along the rain-soaked streets, stopping every so often for a rich, delicious dessert. We watched a German fall into a canal and passed the Bridge of Sighs, which my mother said led directly to the dungeons and afforded the prisoner his last glimpse of Venice, a view which I thought must have been not unlike the one I'd once had while standing in front of the cracked wall.

When we returned to London, Leon jokingly asked how our honeymoon had gone, and then reminded us that there was a kernel of truth to every joke.

Parliament Hill fronted onto the Heath, and every weekend two friends knocked on my door and the three of us would walk to the public courts and play tennis. One day, when I'd just returned from the Heath, I heard the fateful word: Greece. We were all going back to Greece, my mother said. When I turned to Leon and saw the powerfully vacant expression in his eyes, I knew it was true.

Chapter 6

THE MANY-HEADED HYDRA

There were three boats a day from Athens and Leon was there to greet each one, patiently waiting at a portside café for my mother's arrival. I often passed him on my way to and from the beach and sometimes I joined him, as I did now, sipping a Coke and looking out over the harbour with its small fishing boats and yachts moored to the sea floor. Leon drank small cupfuls of black coffee in the morning, ouzo in the afternoon and early evening. It was his serene gaze over the water which I tried to imitate, turning, every so often, my glass of Coke a quarter of the way around, as he did his ouzo.

Our house was only a few minutes away and level with the port, in a village that made a slow rise up the side of a hill. Although Leon hadn't rented it with the ferry in mind, it made it easy for him to come and go.

There was no phone in the house so my mother's arrival, while imminent, was not specific; Leon had been sitting beside his coffees and his ouzos, automatically delivered to his table, for the past two days.

Leon enjoyed the wait. He often arrived a full hour before the boat's arrival and stayed well after the boat had left port. When he wasn't staring at the harbour, he was reading a book. From a distance his black-haired head, rising and falling from one view to the next, looked like the pieces of fruit and other flotsam that gently bobbed up and down in the harbour water.

Hydra had been a compromise — if going to Greece could be considered a compromise — peacefully arranged between Leon and my mother. He'd made it clear that he'd never set foot in Molyvos again, likening it to a dog returning to smell his own shit. He would, however, consider another village, on another island, preferably one that was far away from his last deposit.

Hydra was four hours south of Athens by boat, Molyvos was twelve, in the opposite direction. The island suited Leon because it wasn't Molyvos and it suited my mother because it was still Greece, which was probably why she'd been taken by surprise when he'd declared his wish to leave London early. My mother was caught unprepared — she'd always been the one to rent the house in Greece and ready it for others — and was unable to respond because her passport needed to be renewed. She couldn't leave London, a fact Leon must have known and included in his calculations. If we were all going to Greece, Leon ensured it would first be touched with his steady hand. As an added surprise, he asked if I'd like to join him, to "jump the gun," as he called it. I readily accepted.

During my last week of school Philip White had sat beside me in math class and shown me his switchblade collection. The blades rested in a wooden box lined with velvet, pinned down like butterflies. He stroked the handles and asked me to do the same.

"Some people collect stamps but they're not useful. You can't do anything with them."

I nodded in agreement and asked what he was doing for the summer.

"Nothing much." He smiled, but it was crooked and pointed downward towards his collection.

"And you?"

"I'm going to Greece."

"I'd like to go abroad someday," he said, and I knew he never would. Philip knew it too. "You're lucky, David." He closed the box's lid, told me to have a good time, and walked back to his chair.

At some point during the year I'd forgotten about Philip White and he'd forgotten about me. Eli, too. A month before, when Eli had kicked a new victim into the urinals, the bright sobs had comforted me. I'd been standing only a few feet away but I was no longer the target. I belonged. When I left for Greece with Leon I knew I had a place to come back to.

Leon was still nursing his milky-white glass of ouzo when the boat came into port. This was the part I liked best and the reason I joined him at the table, which remained perfectly still as the engines shuddered in annoyance and the sailors screamed at one another. Large brown ropes were thrown overboard and grabbed by men at the dock who wrapped the noose around huge metal canisters. As the ropes were tightened, people on both sides pushed forward, waiting for the gangplank to be secured.

Leon and I watched the first passengers disembark. The Greeks, familiar with the boat, knew how to reach the front of the line. The tourists followed, one at a time down the plank, dragging luggage behind them. Leon and I waited for my mother, who would most likely be among them. A familiar face appeared, but it wasn't my mother's. Leon rose from his chair and went to greet my father.

"Leon!"

"Irving."

"Son!"

"Dad."

My father took a seat at our table and ordered a coffee. Under more normal circumstances I imagined he would have seen Leon's glass and said something like: "Ah, Leon, I see you're drinking the gods' nectar." He might have referred to its milky sheen, spoken about Homer's light, even mentioned the boat ride; but my father was no longer interested in his own trivialities. He wore a Greek sailor's cap, the band of marine rope strapped around the front peak as strong and purposeful as the ones which moored the ship to its harbour.

"Is Aviva with you?" Leon asked.

It was not a good question. The ship's passengers had all disembarked.

"Is she with me? Isn't she with you?"

"No."

Leon explained about my mother's passport and told him about his patient anticipation at the table while my father organized his coffee cup, moving it from his left side until it sat directly before him. He lifted it to his mouth and took a sip.

"Why are you here, Irving?"

"To see Aviva."

My father's answer was disarmingly direct and put Leon at ease. He laughed.

"So am I, Irving."

"Aviva sent me a letter, saying she wanted to see me.
I didn't expect you to be here."

"I see." Leon twirled his glass. "I didn't expect you
either, Irving."

My father looked at the boat he'd just come off, and
then beyond the boat, to the hotel room he'd booked in
Athens, the plane trip across the Atlantic, the tickets he'd
bought in Montreal.

"Leon," he said, "we've been had."

The two of them seemed content to sit at the table,
my father's luggage touching my leg, and watch the boat
depart for the next island. I wondered, as I'm sure Leon
did, about my mother's letter. Even my mother couldn't
have been this stupid, I thought. Obviously, one of her
letters had gotten through, informing my father of our
decision to visit Hydra, but had she said anything more? My
father could have been lying or, more likely, he'd seen only
what he'd wished to see in the letter. He was a man who
invested words with meaning — it was his profession — and
I sensed that in the end it really didn't matter exactly what
my mother had written. It was my father's interpretation
that mattered. He shaped voices until they could be heard
only by him.

"Where are you staying, Irving?"

This was another bad question. I already knew the
answer and so did Leon.

"With Leonard, up at his house."

"So he's here now? I haven't seen him."

"Leonard's here. I cabled him two days ago."

With that my father lifted himself off his chair,
grabbed his baggage and walked around the port, from left
to right, until he reached its centre, as if he were the coffee
cup and the village, the hand which moved him. Then he
plunged forward and disappeared up the narrow street.

That evening, Leon and I sat at a restaurant and ate in silence, shuttling plates of tzatziki, olives, and feta cheese between us until there was nothing left. On our way back home, we passed more restaurants with outdoor tables, more eaters, whose cries of laughter followed us down the street.

Leon had recognized his mistake, a mistake that must have filled him with wonder: how had he allowed it to happen? Leon had been to Hydra before, stopping at a hotel before moving on; my mother had been to Hydra because of Leonard. We'd stayed with him several times over the years and though my mother hadn't come expecting to see him, Leonard was the one who'd familiarized her with the island. He was indirectly responsible for our present stay. Now that my father was here, it no longer felt even indirect. Now that it was too late for him to do anything about it, Leon realized that another steady hand had reached Greece before him.

As I lay down in bed I had the distinct impression that Leonard and my father were looking down on us from the house up on the hill, another promontory for my father to gaze down upon the world.

There were now two bobbing heads waiting for my mother, one belonging to Leon, the other to my father. They sat at the same portside table. I passed them on my way to breakfast and chose a restaurant further down the harbour. Each day the morning boat from Athens glided into port, the passengers disembarked, the horn blew, and then it sailed off. Leon and my father remained at the table, drinking coffee.

I joined them for the afternoon boat. So did Leonard, who sat between them and looked towards the horizon as if he'd rather have been there. His calm discomfort made me distrust him. He wished to remain in the middle but Leon and my father left very little room for him; he sat on a chair borrowed from another table.

"Well, here we are," my father said, "waiting for our Helen of Troy."

The waiter brought three glasses of ouzo and a Coke to our table. No special alchemy was required for my drink and I watched as Leon, Leonard, and finally my father transformed the clear liquids that lay before them into a cloudy opaque white. They poured the drinks down their throats and ordered more.

Once again the boat pulled into port and once again the ropes were thrown overboard, the engines shuddered, and the gangplank was rolled into position. But this time, when the passengers streamed down the walkway, my mother was among them. When I saw her I realized she was the most beautiful woman I'd ever seen.

I'd spent my days staring at Swedish girls, furtive glances so frequent I wondered if I was developing a nervous tic. Men jumped into the sea just to impress them, from a cliff near the beach. I wouldn't jump for my mother — she didn't look Swedish — but Leon and my father would, already had, and the reason became clear to me as I watched her descend from the boat. It was her eyes. The Swedish girls didn't have eyes like that. Nobody had eyes like that. Their clarity was so great that no alchemist could ever cloud them over.

Leon and my father stood up from the table and walked towards her, standing on either side of the gangplank as my mother hit the ground. It was her turn to be in the middle but she was given even less room than Leonard and, in shock, she simply kept on walking until she reached our table.

Leonard raised his glass of ouzo. "Welcome to Hydra."

My mother and father spent the late mornings walking the narrow footpaths that crisscrossed the small island. I sometimes caught glimpses of them on my way to the beach. Sometimes I saw them while standing on the cliff, as I awaited my turn to jump off into the sea, but still they were always above me, often in front of me, walking to an unknown part of the island.

Leon, meanwhile, sat at his café table, though he no longer had a reason for doing so, and watched the boats from Athens come and go. It was as if by being alone again, he was still waiting for my mother to arrive. She did arrive, every afternoon, though not by boat. I'd see them sitting at a taverna or a restaurant on my way back from the beach.

Since my mother's arrival, Leon and my father no longer saw each other. She shuttled between them, mornings with my father, afternoons and evenings with Leon, pushing them farther and farther apart until she had just enough room to believe that the shouts from one couldn't be heard by the other.

All that happened was that the shouts became louder.

"Are you erotic?"

My father popped a black olive into his mouth, bit into its flesh, and awaited my answer.

It was the afternoon — my father's time off — and I'd found him sitting alone at a taverna, reading. I'd sat down beside him because he was my father and told him about my mother's eyes, how they had no colour because they were of every colour.

"Ah, you've noticed. Aviva has a great talent for life. It's a rare, precious gift."

I wondered what talent my mother could possibly possess when it led to such confusion and unhappiness, unless that in itself was a talent. And that's when he asked me if I was erotic.

I didn't fully understand the question but I understood its terms. To answer yes was to be captivated by my mother's eyes, to answer no was to be blinded by them. It was my fault: I'd mentioned her eyes and been disarmed by my father's remorse over them.

"No," I answered.

My father nodded and then, to my surprise, fell into the trap he'd dug for me.

"Do you think *I'm* erotic?"

I grabbed an olive from the plate and popped it into my mouth.

"No," I answered.

"No? You don't think I'm erotic?"

My father furiously swivelled the olive pit in his mouth while I shook my head.

"Well son, what you don't seem to realize is that I'm a poet. By definition I'm erotic."

My definition was pedestrian, he said. It was earth and not some small portion of its dominion that he found erotic. Its hills were breasts, its grasses tufts of hair. The world was intoxicating, a perfumed boudoir whose sheets were always being changed for the next customer.

"Do you understand?" he demanded.

I said that I did, which was true. We'd both been unable to escape my mother's eyes.

"When is Irving leaving?"

Leon and my mother were taking a stroll along the port. I wasn't far behind, licking an ice cream. "Notice that I'm not even asking why he's here."

"I didn't ask him to come, Leon."

"Notice that I'm not asking why, Aviva."

"Leon, I can't just ask him to leave. This isn't a private island."

Leon shook his head.

"I'm not going to play any more games. I won't fight any longer." But Leon was shouting and it was clear that he *was* fighting. "I've lost enough of my dignity and I can't afford to lose any more."

"I'm exhausted," my mother pleaded, then turned and asked if I'd like to get another ice cream. Knowing she was powerless, I stood my ground.

"That's not an answer," said Leon.

"No, it's not, and you deserve one. Irving still loves me." She quickly raised her hands. "I don't want to live with him any more, Leon. It's just that I feel responsible for his happiness. He's come a long way to see me."

"Do you know what love is, Aviva? If I had to choose between writing a great book and you, I'd put down my pen and never look at it again."

My mother stared at him. She blinked. And then an unmistakable look of contempt spread across her face.

Leon quickened his step: "You'll never learn, Aviva." I thought he was going to walk away but he suddenly stopped, spun around, and faced her.

"Give me your hands."

My mother raised her arms and moved towards him like a sleepwalker, slipping her hands into his and allowing them to be gently rubbed by Leon's long, dark fingers.

"It has to go," he said.

"Don't you dare!"

My mother jerked her hand back but it was too late. The ring was no longer on her finger.

"Give me back my ring!" my mother cried.

Leon held it up to her.

"You were the one who pulled it off, Aviva. I just held onto it."

Then he cast the ring into the blue Aegean.

"My ring!" she yelled. "I've lost my ring!"

But there was a new ring on her finger, a thin white line. My mother saw it too.

EPILOGUE

Leon was in the garden, a pair of clippers in his hands,
inspecting some overly enthusiastic vines he'd planted
the year before, when he heard my mother's call from
inside the house.

"Yoo-hoo, Lee."

Leon chose to ignore my mother and I heard the
wooden floorboards squeak as she moved to another part
of the house. Another two-note greeting then. "Lee?"

I was standing on the deck beneath an orange tree
whose fruit I'd just plucked and squeezed into a glass. It
was hard to believe, standing there in Leon's peaceful
garden, that I was in Los Angeles, but then such a sense of
dislocation was perhaps the essence of the city. Leon loved
everything about this place, had loved it from the moment
he'd first stepped off the plane over ten years ago. In a city
where everything was in motion, Leon had found a home
he never wished to leave and his garden, with its footpaths,
fountains, and stone walls, wasn't meant to block out L.A.

but to help him tend and grow a little piece of it.

"Lee? Leon!"

More squeaks from the floorboards. My mother was moving towards the garden. Although I'd been standing just outside the door for over ten minutes, Leon hadn't heard me come out. A banana tree with wide tropical ferns stood between the two of us, so the mischievous smile which spread across his face could not have been for my benefit. I watched him step into the vines and disappear.

"Yoo-hoo, Leon."

My mother entered the deck from the kitchen. She wasn't far from him but he was camouflaged and she was impatient. I heard her cluck in irritation and then retreat back into the house. Moments later Leon re-emerged, garden clippers in hand, to resume his inspection. I'd once seen a moose soundlessly withdraw into the dense forest and then re-emerge as I moved past; the thrill of both encounters was oddly similar.

The garden was Leon's refuge but not from my mother. This green patch of earth was his offering to her.

Leon had written a book about the garden, about my mother. He'd handed the first published copy of *A Garden Story* to her, and it had made her cry. I hadn't witnessed those tears — I'd been informed of them by a close friend of hers — but I would have found the idea of Leon's garden as a symbol of his love for her a bit precious if it wasn't for his ferocity. I was watching him now, with his shears, ripping out unwanted branches. When it came to his garden, Leon wasn't fucking around.

The orange tree I stood beneath had been the only thing in the garden to have preceded Leon's arrival. It hadn't borne fruit for years and the soil which surrounded it had been hard and barren. Nothing could grow here and nothing had grown here until the day, a year after they'd moved in, that Leon took a pickaxe and began to break up the compressed soil.

Leon had never gardened before and at first he didn't know what to do. Even now, he said, after all these years, it was still an experiment. The year-old vines which he was pruning had been bought on my last visit. Their original habitat had been Australasia, or perhaps southern Africa, I couldn't remember, but they too were part of his experiment. As with my mother's tears, I hadn't been a witness to this transformation of the garden, but I'd never been under the illusion that it was complete. Each visit revealed a new bower of leaves, a new flowering plant, another rivulet of flowing water, and all of it surviving under Leon's protective gaze, which was fiercer than the desert sun.

I heard my mother's voice from the kitchen. She was singing. The ceramic tiles in the kitchen, the wooden floors, the bright clean walls, and all the idiotic things my mother had collected over the years — Tibetan prayer wheels, Mexican figurines — they'd all been beautifully arranged. It wasn't just the garden which was well tended.

My mother, of course, still wished to move – up in the hills, out on the coast, down the street. "You never really recover from house-mania," was Leon's medical prognosis. But recover she had; it was just that, out of habit, my mother liked to scratch even if she no longer itched. Besides, Leon would never have left his garden. "He wants to be buried in it!" my mother confided in me.

Leon moved to another patch of the garden, picked up a hose, and began to douse his plants with water. Flat stones which he had laid down years before cut a path through his garden. Leon had written that his hands had bled as he'd dug out the hard soil and placed them in the ground. The path had preceded the garden; an act of faith.

I stepped off the deck and passed Leon who raised his eyebrows in greeting and continued with his watering. Though I never felt unwelcome in his garden, I always had the sense that I was intruding, and I wondered if my mother, whose presence this garden owed its existence to, ever felt the same way.

My mother was still singing and her voice mingled with the ripple of running water from one of Leon's latest acquisitions – a statue of a little boy peeing into a ceramic bowl. Other items, including a cut-out of a cow, a stop sign, and several old kitchen bowls had been collected and assembled in the garden with the same sense of order as my mother's trinkets inside the house. I knew it was just a cheap knock-off, but there was something affecting about the little boy, something beautiful in the tilt of his head and in his white rounded belly.

"There you are!" My mother stepped into the garden and wagged her finger.

Leon turned towards her and smiled.

"There's no hiding from me, Leon."

A tangle of plant cuttings lay at Leon's feet but my mother stepped over them, kicking a few twigs out of the way.

"My wild gardener," she said. And I watched as they embraced each other beneath the green canopy that Leon had planted all those years ago.

My father was pissing against the wall. It was a wooden wall, part of a boathouse, freshly painted and trimmed for the summer season and fully exposed to the family of four who were pushing off from the dock. The two children, who were sitting up front, wore bright red life-vests strapped across their upper bodies. They also wore baseball caps, the crisp peaks protruding straight ahead like dog snouts.

It was late morning, with fast-moving clouds over-head, but it seemed to me that a steady shaft of light illu-minated my father and bathed him in its warmth. The light silvered his thatch of grey hair and brightened his dark brown pants. The pants of an old man, I thought. If those dog snouts sniffed my father out, the whole family would be party to a pathetic sight; an elderly man, suffering from the indignity of age, urinating in public.

My father's broad back was turned away from all of us; he was engulfed by his own needs. Old age had not diminished his bulk. With legs set wide apart he was a sturdy figure, unaware of his own actions, uninterested in the actions of others. The marina, though small, must have possessed a toilet, but my father had chosen to piss against a wall in full view of whoever happened to pass by.

We — my wife, my father, and I — were staying at a luxury hotel which had provided us with packed lunches for our afternoon excursion. Those lunches, along with a fishing rod, picnic blanket, and pillow for my father to sit on, were now in the boat. For my father such details, or rather the organizing principle behind such details, were, I knew, relegated to the realm of abstraction. He was here in the woods and he needed to pee. What did he know from toilets?

I was sure his action wasn't a case of mental infir-mity, but rather a case of elementary logic; he'd chosen the most exposed wall of the boathouse precisely because it was the most convenient place to relieve himself. This, I knew, did not constitute a rupture with the past, but rather an aggressive continuity: my father was a man who pissed where he wanted to.

Zorba's words came to me as I stood there on the dock, life-vest in hand. "What is life, Boss, if not to pull down your pants and look for trouble?" For the first time, I could hear the threat lurking behind those words. My father wasn't looking for trouble any more than Zorba was. He was declaring his freedom.

If my father's actions were somehow poetic, then mine were decidedly prosaic: I was embarrassed. The potential for embarrassment was all around me, not just here in the marina, but in my daily life. I always searched for toilets, never jumped a queue, dressed in an appropriate fashion, and rarely insulted those whom I disliked or even, for that matter, those who disliked me. Try as I might, I couldn't quite convince myself that my politeness was based on compassion. My behaviour was far too reactive. I hated the people in the boat, for instance, but I cared what they thought of my father.

"My father's peeing in public," I whispered to Annie, who was sitting in the boat, making last-minute adjustments for our trip on the lake.

"He's what?"

"Look," I said.

By now my father was absentmindedly buckling up his pants.

"Irving, it's time to get into the boat."

"Is it time to go?" he asked.

"It was for you."

"Marvellous!"

He sauntered down the pier towards us, the wooden boards creaking under his weight.

My father peered into the boat and, spying the lunch boxes, bellowed, "What's for lunch?"

"Keep your hands off, Irving," my wife responded. But it wasn't just my wife responding; it was all his wives. The rules were obviously replicable. First you asked, then you were denied. My father enjoyed both the start and the finish of this game. There were other rules of course, darker ones, but they emerged later.

I helped my father into the boat. When he had one leg planted on the dock and the other trying to secure itself in the boat, I noticed that his fly was undone. There was also a dark stain on his pants. As we began our journey down the narrow channel that led into the lake, I wondered how it had come to pass that my father could piss in public and that I'd be the one to feel desperately inadequate.

This latest visit with my father had come about almost by default. Since Annie had to travel to Quebec City for her work, I had decided to drive to Montreal and spend some time with him. I'd pick Annie up at the airport when she had finished working, and then we'd all drive up to the luxury resort which belonged to the company she worked for and have a wonderful few days together.

I arrived at my father's house in a car.

"A car!" he exclaimed, coming out to the porch when I first arrived. He walked down the steps and slid his hand back and forth across the car's metallic finish, an act which was altogether unusual for a man who couldn't have distinguished a belching Skoda from a Mercedes and wouldn't have wanted to even if the opportunity had ever presented itself.

"Is this your car?"

I nodded.

"You own this car?" He was impressed.

His attention seemed to increase the car's width and height with every passing second. This machine, parked in my father's driveway, pointed to something impressive about both the car and its owner.

"You *own* this car?" he asked again.

Inside, the cool air of my father's house managed to deflate my momentary importance and restore its proper perspective. It wasn't just the cool air which aided this process, but also the furnishings which, like the house itself, were stolid. One of the first things I saw as I entered was my father's brown upholstered couch, which had become uniformly stained over the decades. There was an off-white carpet on the floor, a few bookcases, a painting or two on the walls, and an armchair.

I knew that chair well from our previous houses. It was from this chair that my father would lay bare the world in all its foul glory, while I lay prostrate on the couch, the afternoon sun warming my legs even in the dead of winter. In my father's estimation the world was in ill health. It exuded a rotten stench into the atmosphere. Humanity, he assured me, was a cosmic fart. Not even cosmic; it was just a fart.

I caught sight of a blue stone on the mantelpiece. Marooned in my father's house, it quivered with delight, a blue lagoon. The stone had belonged to my mother, and once I'd locked eyes on it other artifacts, small but significant, came into view — erotic statues from India, some pottery fragments from Greece, a chunk of ivory.

These pieces had once been part of a larger collection which had followed us from house to house. There were dancing Indian whores whirling beside bright Afghan rugs, Balinese monkey masks casting lurid looks towards Moroccan teapots. There was even a beanbag, made from strips of multicoloured leather, that would periodically release the peculiar smell of Middle Asia, a dry odour of straw and dust.

Most of these objects had followed my mother to Hollywood and were now placed on whitewashed walls, perched beside flowering cactus and hibiscus, all washed clean by the light of southern California. The few artifacts which had remained with my father had also done surprisingly well; his neglect had allowed them to flourish.

When Alla, my father's daytime housekeeper, came into the room and offered me a cup of tea, my father used this opportunity to slip upstairs to take a nap.

"How is he?" I asked.

Alla sighed and then shrugged her shoulders.

"He needs care. I have to make sure that there is someone in the house all the time."

I scratched my nose.

"Your father is a genius and such men should never have children. What can a man like him do with children? It is impossible."

I sat in my father's chair and nodded sagely. The fingers of my hands were interlocked and rested on my belly, the very posture my father adopted when facing bad and potentially dangerous news.

Apart from a few brief but cordial conversations over the phone, Alla and I had never met. She was from eastern Europe and masked her present discomfort by being stern and tidy. After pouring the tea, she refused to let me get the milk carton from the fridge. Instead, my milk arrived in a small ceramic jug.

"Your father loves you," she said.

My fingers began to twitch.

Alla's judgments weren't directed solely at me. I had the impression that she reserved her fiercest pronouncements for those she barely knew: the next-door neighbour, a friend's grandson, perhaps a politician or two. She wasn't about to lay blame either on the man she took care of — and obviously admired — or on that man's son, who now sat opposite her. Her censure was directed towards something far more intangible and hence blameless: genius.

"When you call," Alla went on, "you cannot imagine his joy. 'Alla,' he shouts to me, 'do you know who just phoned me? My son!' 'I know, Irving,' I tell him. 'It's your son!'"

Alla looked at me. "He's like this all day."

And as if to prove her point, she repeated their exchange one more time. This time when she shouted, "I know, Irving!" I could hear the impatience in her voice.

What, I wondered, was Alla telling me? That my father loved me and enjoyed getting telephone calls from me but, as a genius, shouldn't have had me in the first place? Actually, that was close. My father loved me and enjoyed hearing from me, *despite* being a genius. I could tell Alla found her answer satisfying; having a generous heart, her wish was to offer me some of her contentment.

If asked, Alla, I suspected, would have been hard pressed to describe genius. Could she ever have thought it possible that genius would reside in an old man who relied on her for toilet rolls and coffee beans? Luckily, my father helped clarify matters. He made it clear that he was, indeed, a genius, and despite his present fragility, it must have been hard to ignore his conviction. There were books he could point to, many with his face on the cover. When dusting, Alla would surely have pulled a book or two out of their slots, and seen for herself the accolades printed on the jackets.

Then there were the letters. By and large these letters didn't conform to anything Alla was familiar with. They were neither the personal letters sent by friends, nor the impersonal ones received from her bank or phone company. Instead, these letters were a kind of hybrid: personal notes sent by institutions.

The people behind these letters, many of them important in their own right, wanted to spend time with my father, a fact which must have greatly impressed Alla. She not only spent a great deal of time with him — he actually paid her for the privilege.

Making a living from the goings-on in one's head was unnatural, even somewhat unclean. I had always thought so, and I was sure Alla felt the same way. Such occupations inevitably led to the kind of familial mess she now saw before her: the distant son, the faint echo of a previous wife.

Alla stood up to answer the knock on the door. It was my wife arriving from Quebec City. I had forgotten all about her; half an hour in my father's house and it was hard to imagine that I had a wife.

"Who's there?" It was my father, yelling from his bedroom.

"It's your son's wife," Alla shouted back.

"Who?"

"Your son's wife. Your daughter-in-law, Irving."

We waited for him as he made himself presentable, and then after the greetings were made, Annie excused herself and disappeared up the stairs.

"Where's she going?" my father asked.

"To the bathroom," I answered.

"Is she coming back?" He looked worried.

"Yes, she's coming back," I assured him. "Don't worry, we won't be bereft of women."

It had been my intention to take my father into the city later that afternoon, sit him down for a smoked-meat sandwich, and generally "get him out of the house," as

Annie put it. But already I felt listless and immensely sorry for myself. Why the fuck was I here?

That evening as Annie and I lay on the pull-out couch in the basement, she whispered to me, "It's good that we're taking your father on a trip. He needs to get out." As if to massage the words into my body, she gently rubbed my forearm with her hand.

This then was the acceptable answer for why I was here: my father needed me, even if he didn't know why.

My wife sat in the front of the boat, my father in the middle. I was in the back, clutching the handle of the small outboard motor. I was in control, guiding us all to some rocky outcrop in the middle of the lake. To further heighten my sense of omnipotence, I'd occasionally reduce the boat's speed, let the waves punch the metal hull, and then open up the throttle.

It was too noisy to talk in the boat, so my father sat there, head thrust pugnaciously foward, nose sniffing the winds. I felt as if I were transporting Churchill across the Canadian Shield.

My father, I knew, was having a wonderful time, his delight compounded by the mystery of it all. He'd been unsure as to how I'd managed to deliver him to this place, or even how I'd landed on his doorstep in Montreal, but now that he was here, he was determined to enjoy himself.

When we reached the island, I helped my father out of the boat and ensured that he was firmly planted on the ground before letting go of him. While he stretched his legs and commented favourably on the scenery, I scooped up the remaining objects from the boat and tightened the mooring ropes. Then I pointed my father in the necessary direction.

Annie was already at a clearing we had seen on our approach to the island, and my father and I followed the narrow trail that led towards her. As he worked his way along the dirt path, flicking the narrow branches away from his face, he suddenly tripped and fell to the ground with a loud thud.

Winded and confused, he still managed to lift his left hand off the ground and wave me away when I reached down to help him. All things considered, this must have taken a sizable amount of energy. Behind him and partly covered by soil lay the culprit – an exposed tree root no larger than a twig.

As he lay there, I noticed for the first time that he was wearing sandals, an article of clothing I usually associated with children, not with old men. His exposed feet looked vulnerable and somehow sad.

"Well, my boy, they must have it in for me." It was as close to a whisper as my father was capable of. "At my age even a twig is treacherous."

My father was no longer staring at the ground which had felled him, but at the heavens which had offended him.

"You miserable bastard," he said, staring up at the sky. There was a slight grin on his face and, as he began to hoist himself up, he looked enormous, a man of thunderous prominence.

He crashed through the forest and made his way out to the clearing, where Annie had set out the picnic.

"So," I heard him say to my wife as he sat down and grabbed a chicken leg, "how's your plumbing?"

"David, wake up."

These words, whispered into my ear, were immediately followed by an insistent prodding of my back with her finger. My head was partly submerged under a pillow, but the pale light of early morning managed to seep through. When I opened my eyes, the first thing I noticed was how white the hotel sheets were.

On Annie's silent orders, I turned over and found my father standing a few feet from the foot of the bed, fully dressed and clean-shaven but without shoes or socks.

"He's just staring at us," Annie said quietly.

"Dad?" The door adjoining our two rooms was wide open and lay almost directly behind him. A corner of his bed was visible, as was the antique writing table tucked up against the window.

"What a beautiful image! Dark hair on one pillow, blond on the other. Light and dark. Beautiful."

I propped myself up against the bed frame and stared at my father's exposed feet and then at my own.

"I don't know where I am," he said.

"You're in the hotel."

"Your room is right behind you, Irving," Annie said.

A quick turn of his head and the look of confusion briefly left his face.

"The both of you are a magnificent creation. Adam and Eve."

"Are you ready for some breakfast?" Annie asked.

"Who are you?" he asked.

"This is Annie. My wife."

My father looked down at his bare feet, then at me.

"Who are *you*?"

"I'm your son," I said. "David."

The typeface used throughout the book is Mrs. Eaves,

an historical revival based on the design of Baskerville.

Mrs. Eaves was designed in 1996 by Zuzana Licko.

The typeface is named after Sarah Eaves.

As John Baskerville was setting up his printing and type

business, Mrs. Eaves moved in with him as a live-in

housekeeper, eventually becoming his wife after the

death of her first husband. Like the widows of

Caslon and Bodoni and the daughters of Fournier,

Sarah completed the printing of the unfinished

volumes that John Baskerville left upon his death.

Photographs courtesy of Aviva Whiteson

Book design by Paul Hodgson, Spencer Francey Peters

Typesetting by Marie Jircik